WILEY SMALL BUSINESS EDITIONS

Jeffrey G. Allen, *Complying with the ADA*

Kim Baker and Sunny Baker, *How to Promote, Publicize, and Advertise Your Growing Business*

Fred Hahn, *Do-It-Yourself Advertising*

Daryl Allen Hall, *1001 Businesses You Can Start from Home*

Herman Holtz, *How to Start and Run a Writing and Editing Business*

John Kremer, *The Complete Direct Marketing Sourcebook: A Step-by-Step Guide to Organizing and Managing a Successful Direct Marketing Program*

Gregory and Patricia Kishel, *How to Start, Run, and Stay in Business*

Gregory and Patricia Kishel, *Build Your Own Network Sales Business*

Gregory and Patricia Kishel, *Cashing In on the Consulting Boom*

Gregory and Patricia Kishel, *Start, Run, and Profit from Your Own Home-Based Business*

Christopher Malburg, *Business Plans to Manage Day-to-Day Operations*

Harry J. McLaughlin, *The Entrepreneur's Guide to Building a Better Business: A Step-by-Step Approach*

Patrick D. O'Hara, *How to Computerize Your Small Business*

Richard L. Porterfield, *Insider's Guide to Winning Government Contracts*

M. John Storey, *Taking Money Out of Your Corporation*

L. Perry Wilbur, *Money in Your Mailbox: How to Start and Operate a Successful Mail-Order Business, Second Edition*

M.G.A. More Good Accounts   The M.G.A. GAIN
GAIN Growing Assets + Insurance Numbers Program

OTHER BOOKS BY ROBERT W. BLY

Creative Careers: Real Jobs in Glamour Fields (with Gary Blake)

Elements of Business Writing (with Gary Blake)

Selling Your Services: Proven Strategies for Getting Clients to Hire You (or Your Firm)

Keeping Clients Satisfied: Make Your Service Business More Successful and Profitable

Advertising Manager's Handbook

Targeted Public Relations: How to Get Thousands of Dollars of Free Publicity for Your Product

The Elements of Technical Writing (with Gary Blake)

THE PERFECT SALES PIECE

A Complete Do-It-Yourself Guide to Creating Brochures, Catalogs, Fliers, and Pamphlets

Robert W. Bly

John Wiley & Sons, Inc.

New York • Chichester • Brisbane • Toronto • Singapore

Copyright © 1994 by Robert W. Bly
Published by John Wiley & Sons, Inc.

Portions of this book previously appeared in Create the Perfect Sales Piece, © 1985 by John Wiley & Sons, Inc.

Library of Congress Cataloging-in-Publication Data:

Bly, Robert W.
   The perfect sales piece : a complete do-it-yourself guide to creating brochures, catalogs, fliers, and pamphlets / Robert W. Bly.
      p. xxxx cm.— (Wiley small business editions)
   "Portions of this book previously appeared in Create the perfect sales piece, c1985"—T.p. versa.
   ISBN 0-471-00403-0 (cloth) – – – 0-471-00411-1 (paper)
      Includes bibliographical references and index.
      1. Advertising, Direct-mail.   2. Commercial catalogs.   3. Advertising fliers,   4. Pamphlets.
   I. Bly, Robert W. Create the perfect sales piece.   II. Title.   III. Series.
   HF5861.857   1994
   659.13'3--dc20   94-11311

Printed in the United States
10 9 8 7 6 5 4 3 2 1

To Marc Garfinkle
a true friend

ACKNOWLEDGMENTS

There are three groups of people who helped make this book a reality, and I'd like to thank all of them.

First, there are those advertising professionals who specialize in creating successful promotional literature: Steve Brown, Arnie Diskin, Harry Moshier, Grant Faurot, Bonnie Blake, Mary Ciccita, Gill Roessner, Ken Weissman, Leslie Klein, John Alexander, Rick Hibberd, Andrea Nicoll, Kent Martin, Maria Harvey, Martha Eckert, Diane Lazelle, Valerie Rasines, Anne Rooney, and others too numerous to mention. Working with these people has taught me a lot about design, copywriting, and production.

Second, I thank the people and organizations who have graciously permitted me to reproduce examples of their work in this book:

Associated Air Freight
Barrett, Haentjens & Co.
The BOC Group
Stephen M. Brown
Caterpillar Lift Truck
Crane Co., Chempump Division
Susie Dugaw
George Duncan
Emery Printing Co.
English Heritage Antiques
René Gnam
W. L. Gore & Associates, Inc.
IBM
Herschell Gordon Lewis
Mars Mineral Corporation
Navta Associates, Inc.
Stanley J. Robens
Rosemont Inc.

Finally, thanks to my editor, PJ Dempsey, for making this book much better than it was when it first crossed her desk, and to Ruth Cavin, Elizabeth Morse-Cluley, and Alan Ross for their helpful comments and suggestions.

CONTENTS

PREFACE

Just about every company in business today needs some type of printed literature to establish credibility and provide information on its products or services. And because it's your job (or part of your job) to create this material, you bought this book.

The Perfect Sales Piece provides step-by-step instructions for every phase of the job—from evaluating what type of sales literature you need, to planning and outlining your brochure, writing and design, finding illustrations and photographs, creating mechanicals, and printing.

The Perfect Sales Piece tells you how to create printed literature that fits your product, your company, your image, and your budget. It can guide you in producing anything from a $100,000, 32-page corporate capabilities brochure to a $10 offset flier that will be posted on the local community bulletin board.

Here's how the book is organized:

Chapter 1 sets the stage. It discusses why companies need sales literature, including its benefits and applications, and it describes the 11 basic categories of sales literature.

Chapters 2–4 show you how to set a production schedule and budget for the project and how to decide what information to include in the brochure. You'll also learn where to find and how to work with professional copywriters, photographers, illustrators, graphic artists, desktop publishing services, and printers.

Chapters 5–9 take you through the process of designing, writing, illustrating, and printing your brochure. We also take a look at a number of special problems that may come up in the creation of promotional literature and how to solve them.

Chapter 10 is a guide to managing a *program* of successful promotional literature. It is for the person who plans to produce a whole series of brochures, not just one. You'll also learn how to gauge the success of your literature program.

The book is illustrated with numerous annual reports, product brochures, fliers, booklets, circulars, catalogs, bulletins, newsletters, and mailers. These samples are included to show you what works in design and layout—and what doesn't.

If you have produced a brochure or promo piece you are particularly proud of, why not send it to me so I can share it with readers of the next edition of this book? You will receive full credit, of course. Write to:

Bob Bly
Copywriter/Consultant
22 E. Quackenbush Avenue, 3rd Floor
Dumont, NJ 07628
(201) 385-1220

CHAPTER ONE

SO YOU THINK YOU NEED PRINTED LITERATURE!

A stockbroker phones a prospect to explain a new investment opportunity. The prospect is mildly interested but isn't ready to take the plunge. "Send me some literature on the fund," says the would-be investor, "and I'll give you a call when I'm ready to spend."

An executive secretary walks into her local delicatessen. "I want you to cater our company's sales meeting next month," she explains to the counterman. "Do you have a catering menu I can take with me to show my boss?"

A management consultant visits a major insurance company and is asked for his client list, schedule of fees, and business card.

We live in a world of documentation, of paper, of establishing credibility. A friendly smile and a handshake aren't enough. We like to feel that we are dealing with people who are established in business, in the same way we prefer a brand name over brand X.

Of course, no amount of fancy brochures, business cards, streamlined logos, or colorful catalogs can guarantee that a job will be done well or that a product won't stop working five minutes after it has been purchased. Still, promotional literature does go a long way toward setting a professional business tone, one that adds a sense of credibility and stability to a business enterprise.

It isn't surprising to find that some of the best-established businesses have the most uniform and attractive sales literature. A certain sureness of tone and style comes with practice.

For example, one of the finest old inns in the United States, the Publick House in Sturbridge, Massachusetts, has a folder in each guest room containing no fewer than 12 brochures—each dealing with a service or element of the inn's features. The brochures contain the Publick House logo, and each is characterized by a similarity of tone and a warm-spirited, low-key approach.

The Publick House has been in business for 200 years. Not every business has had the opportunity to hone its image for that period of time. Yet almost every business requires some form of sales literature to keep products and services in the customer's mind, to distinguish itself from the competition, and to answer a prospective buyer's questions.

A Brochure Can Do Many Things

Most organizations discover the need for printed literature as they conduct their daily business. Frequent requests for brochures force the seller to produce a booklet or flier to satisfy the customers' thirst for information.

But a brochure can do more than fill space in a customer's shopping bag or desk drawer. When executed and used correctly, your brochure can become a powerful tool for promoting your business.

Specifically, a brochure can:

- Inform
- Educate
- Build image
- Establish credibility
- Sell (or help sell) a product or service
- Screen prospects
- Add value

In its most basic role, a brochure is a vehicle for providing information to prospects, customers, and others who want to know more about your product, process, program, system, service, company, idea, or plan. The brochure can be used to provide a basic education for the uninformed or to answer the specific questions a more knowledgeable prospect is likely to ask.

A brochure can also build image and establish credibility. Anybody can have business cards printed for $10 and claim to be a company. But a sales brochure establishes immediate credibility and says to your prospects, "This is a *real* business, not a fly-by-night organization."

According to a study from Thomas Publishing, publishers of one of the country's largest industrial product directories, *90 percent* of all buyers in industry say they must see some type of "printed literature" before they put a product's manufacturer on their approved vendor list. In today's highly competitive business world, producing printed literature has become a necessity, not just a promotional stunt.

By making deliberate choices about the look, quality, and tone of your brochure, you can transmit an image to the reader. A slick, glossy brochure packed with attractive color photographs conveys an image of size, prosperity, and corporate professionalism. But a black-and-white flier on ordinary offset paper may be more appropriate for a company that exterminates roaches and rats.

A brochure can do even more than give information and build image. With strong copy that stresses the benefits and advantages of a product or service, the brochure can be as effective a sales tool as an ad, TV commercial, or direct-mail campaign.

In addition to pulling in the right prospects, literature can weed out the wrong ones. Let's face it: Your product or service isn't for everyone. Some buyers can't afford your price; other buyers are better off with a different type of product. Literature that defines the applications and limitations of your product or service screens out those inquiries that don't represent real prospects. And screening leads with a brochure is a lot cheaper than making sales calls.

Promotional literature can add value to the product or service itself. For example, a purchasing agent may buy one brand of ball bearings over another, not because the first product is any better, but because the first manufacturer's catalog makes it easier to specify and order the bearings. In the same way, a well-written instruction manual for software is often more critical a factor in the product's success than the software itself.

And industrial manufacturers are not the only ones who need brochures. Practically every business and organization—service firms, retailers, consultants, free-lancers, educational institutions, trade associations, publishers—can benefit from describing their operations in printed form.

Five ways to put promotional literature to work

Smart business people don't just sit down and write a brochure. They first think about how they're going to use the brochure: who will read it, what it is designed to accomplish, and how it fits into the sales process.

Not every brochure serves the same function. For example, let's say you sell furnaces. You might have two separate brochures. The first describes the general benefits and nontechnical features of your furnace and is used to generate initial interest in the product at the beginning of the sales process. The second brochure is filled with detailed technical specifications. It answers every question a contractor might have. It is used at the end of the sales process, when the homeowner has pretty much made a decision but wants to check with a trusted expert before shelling out $2,500 for your furnace. The first brochure starts the selling process; the second helps close it.

Here are five ways in which you can put promotional literature to work for your firm:

1. As a leave-behind

As its name implies, a *leave-behind* is a piece of literature that you leave after a meeting with your prospect. A door-to-door encyclopedia salesperson, for example, probably won't close the sale with one visit. If colorful folders describing the encylopedia are left behind, families can study this material at their leisure and make a decision without the pressure created by the presence of a salesperson.

Using a leave-behind ensures that the prospect knows where to reach you because the brochure includes your name, address, and phone number. Moreover, the leave-behind literature helps the prospect to recall the gist of your sales pitch.

2. For inquiry-fulfillment

When I was an advertising manager, our company's advertising and publicity campaign generated 19,000 inquiries a year. Obviously, we couldn't call all those people or visit them personally. So we mailed product brochures to give them the information they asked for.

The brochure was only part of the inquiry fulfillment package. We also sent a sales letter encouraging the prospect to contact our local area representative. And we included an order form, reply card, or other device the prospect could use to let us know her or his level of interest.

Mailing a brochure is the sensible first step in responding to advertising inquiries. Many people who inquire are only marginally interested, or maybe the product isn't right for them. The brochure lets you make contact with these folks for much less than the cost of a phone call or sales visit. Even the serious prospects may want to read a brochure in privacy before deciding whether it's worthwhile to call you, see your salesperson, or visit your store.

One way to increase inquiries from your advertising is to highlight the offer of the free literature in the copy. Instead of just printing your logo and address, say, "The tax-saving benefits of this new bond offering are described in a free, informative pamphlet, 'How to Invest Profitably in Municipal Bonds.' To receive your copy without cost or obligation, write or call us today."

add ons & leave behinds

If a brochure is to be used in inquiry fulfillment, be sure to give it a title that will make people want to send for it. Instead of the title, "Telecommunications Equipment and Services," call the brochure "How to Cut Your Long Distance Phone Bills by 50% or More." More people will send for your literature if they think it contains useful information instead of just straight sales talk.

3. As direct mail

Direct mail is a fast, efficient way of transmitting news to current customers and prospecting for new ones.

A manufacturer of office equipment maintains a computerized mailing list of people who have purchased equipment from the company. The manufacturer mails everyone on the list a different sales flier every month. Each month's flier announces a new product or a special sale on supplies and accessories for the old products.

An engineering firm wants to tell plant managers about its new inspection and maintenance service for wastewater treatment equipment. The company sends out a direct-mail package consisting of a letter, pamphlet, and reply card. The letter introduces the service and highlights the cost savings it offers to industrial plants. The pamphlet gives detailed facts on how the service works and what type of equipment it covers.

There's an old saying among direct-mail marketers: "The letter sells, the brochure tells." In a mailing package, the letter makes the sales pitch, and the brochure gives complete details and illustrates the product with drawings and photos.

Not every mailing requires a brochure. If your mailing is designed to generate sales leads, you can send a letter only and offer the brochure to readers who respond to the letter. If you're selling a product by mail order, you want to give complete details and should include a circular or illustrated folder.

If the product is familiar and easily understood, a letter may be all you need. But if it is unfamiliar, complex, or needs to be shown, include literature with your mailing.

4. As a point-of-sale display

Many merchants display racks of sales literature at the place the product or service is sold. Visit a travel agent's office and you'll find dozens of colorful pamphlets describing faraway places. Stop in at the local bank and you can pick up informative folders on CDs, IRAs, KEOGHs, money markets, and

Nov. 29/05 Tues. Trade Shows - booth promotions.

other profitable investments. Ask your insurance agent about a new policy and he is likely to have a brochure on the policy sitting in a wall rack.

Point-of-sale literature, more so than any other type, must have an attractive, attention-grabbing cover that causes it to stand out in the literature rack and compels the casual browser to pick up the brochure and keep it. Colorful photos or illustrations help; so do powerful headlines that tell a story.

5. As an additional sales tool

We're all familiar with the Avon lady and her sample case, as well as the door-to-door encyclopedia or vacuum cleaner salesperson. But did you know that salespeople play a major role in selling hundreds of other products—everything from machine parts and management seminars to chemical equipment and computers?

These salespeople depend on sales literature to do part of the selling job for them. Not only can literature educate the prospect in advance of the salesperson's visit, but it can help the salesperson make the presentation.

There are three reasons why sales literature is so handy to have around.

First, no salesperson can remember every fact about the product. So the salesperson can use the literature as a *memory aid*. Some salespeople keep the brochure open during their presentation and use it to guide them through the pitch. Others turn to it for occasional reference or to look up answers to difficult questions.

Second, brochures with photos, charts, graphs, and drawings serve to *illustrate the sales pitch*. The salesperson can't bring a company's forklift to the prospective buyer in a warehouse, but *can* bring a brochure with color photographs of it. If the buyer asks a question about the forklift's consumption of electric power, the salesperson can turn to page 5 and show a graph that compares battery charge versus time in use.

Third, sales literature adds *believability* to sales presentations. Some buyers who would question a salesperson's statements will accept a printed sales argument as gospel. As publisher Edward Uhlan explains in his autobiography, *The Rogue of Publishers' Row*, "The reverence people have for the printed word is amazing. Simply because a man appears in print, the public assumes that he has something authoritative to say."

Uhlan was talking about newspaper articles and books, but the principle applies to promotional literature as well. Committing your sales arguments to print will hasten their acceptance by your customers and prospects.

The 11 Basic Types of Promotional Literature

Most sales literature falls into one of the 11 categories listed here:

1. Annual report

The annual report summarizes a company's performance for the past year and promises great things for the year ahead.

Annual reports are generally divided into two parts. The first tells the company's story in narrative form. For large firms, this narrative might consist of several separate subsections, each devoted to one of the firm's various operating companies, divisions, or subsidiaries. The second part, sometimes called the management discussion, consists mainly of numbers reported by the corporation's accounting firm. These numbers tell the story of the firm's financial fitness to those people who understand such things.

The annual report is aimed at a number of audiences, including stockholders, the financial community (especially analysts), vendors, customers, employees, and the business community in general. It also has a number of different purposes: to convince current stockholders to hold on to their shares; to induce potential investors to buy the company's stock; to present an overview of the firm's activities to journalists, employees, prospective employees, vendors, customers, and others who need to know; and to enhance the firm's image.

Do you need an annual report? Not if your business is small or privately held or if the scope of your product line and your organization chart are fairly simple.

When your company goes public, when your business activities are diverse and complex, when your company grows large and spreads across the country or the world—*then* you might consider an annual report.

2. Booklet

The dictionary defines *booklet* as a small bound book. In a promotional sense, a booklet is printed matter that gives *useful information*. In this respect it is different from the brochure, which is written to give *sales information*.

One moving firm publishes a sales brochure titled *Jenkins Movers—The Name You Can Trust*. The brochure contains a blatant sales pitch for Jenkins Movers. Another company, Consolidated Movers, publishes a booklet titled *A Moving Checklist—What to Do Before the Van Arrives*. The booklet contains useful tips on organizing, packing, and planning for a move.

People thinking of a future move send for the informative booklet and keep it on file. When it comes time to move, they find the booklet in their files. They call the publisher, Consolidated Movers, and Consolidated gets the job.

As you can see, there are several advantages to publishing informative booklets. People are more likely to respond to your ad or pick literature from your rack if it contains useful information. And people are also more likely to keep it around. Also, by providing free information, you are perceived as friendly and helpful rather than as a pushy salesperson. Direct mail packages offering free booklets to those who respond can generate response rates of 2 to 7 percent or more.

3. Brochure

A brochure has two jobs: 1) to explain how a product or service works, and 2) to sell the product to the reader by highlighting its advantages, benefits, and applications. There are three basic types of brochures: product, service, and capabilities.

The product brochure can describe either a single product or a product line. The brochure tells what the product is, how it is put together, what it is made of, how it works, what it can do, why it is better than similar products, and what sizes, models, and accessories are available.

The service brochure describes a service offered, such as accounting services, legal services, consulting services, or inspection services. The brochure explains what the service is, why you need it, how it works, and the methods used to perform the service.

The capabilities brochure—also known as the *corporate* or *company* brochure—gives an overview of a company and its capabilities. The brochure explains what the company does, how big it is, what resources it has, and how it is organized. A corporate brochure is like an annual report without the financial section, but it is written to be used for several years instead of just the current year.

Brochures come in all shapes and sizes, but two formats are most common.

The first is the *slim-jim*, which is designed to fit in a standard number 10 business envelope. The slim-jim usually has between four and eight pages and is formed by taking a large piece of paper and folding it into multiple panels (See Figure 1.1). Slim-jims are used when there is not a lot of information to be conveyed, when the company wants to save money on mailing costs, or when the brochure is to be displayed in a literature rack.

Figure 1.1 This "slim-jim" brochure is made by folding an 8½″ × 11″ sheet of paper twice vertically so that it can fit into a standard business envelope.

The second standard format is the brochure with full-size (8½″ × 11″) pages. A brochure will typically have from four to eight pages, although it can be bigger if the product is unusually complex or detailed.

The four-page brochure is formed by folding an 11″ × 17″ sheet of paper in half; the eight-page brochure is formed by stapling two four-pagers together at the fold.

Unlike the booklet, which is merely informative, the brochure must also be *persuasive*. It must sell the reader on the product by highlighting the product's benefits. A good brochure gives the reader many reasons for buying your product instead of another. These can include quality, cost, service, maintenance, efficiency, energy savings, and product performance.

4. Case history

A case history is a product success story. It tells how a customer saved money, solved problems, or improved her or his life by using a product or service.

Each year, thousands of case histories are published as magazine articles, ads, brochures, and publicity releases. Experienced marketers know that case histories make powerful promotions for a number of reasons.

First, people believe in them more than they believe in the regular type of advertising. In a conventional brochure, the manufacturer has to beat its own drum by extolling the virtues of its product. In a case history bulletin, the customer does your selling for you. Furthermore, prospects are more likely to believe this third-party endorsement than your own self-serving claims.

Second, case histories make interesting reading. They tell a story, one that deals with problems similar to those the reader is facing. People relate to case histories because case histories speak directly to their own lives and business situations.

Third, by their very nature, case histories deal with specifics: who had the problem, what the problem was, how the person decided what to do about it, how the product solved it, and the results of buying the product. Such specifics are far more believable and persuasive than the vague generalities that pepper so much of today's lamentable advertising copy.

Detailed case histories may serve as the basis for separate pieces of product literature. And summaries of these case histories, or specific facts or quotations from them, can be woven into your other literature.

5. Catalog

Whereas a brochure is usually restricted to a single product or product line, a catalog is a comprehensive directory of all of a company's products. There are two basic types of catalogs: *mail order* and *industrial.*

Mail-order catalogs offer merchandise the consumer can order directly by mail. They give complete information on each product, including size, price, weight, colors, and materials available. Photos are used to show consumers what they are getting for their money. Mail-order catalogs also contain order forms and postage-paid reply envelopes to make it easy for the customer to order.

Industrial catalogs contain descriptions of products sold to business and industry. The readers of industrial catalogs include purchasing agents, plant managers, engineers, and others who buy such equipment. The catalog descriptions stress technical details, such as safety factors, quality, precision, utility, maintenance and repair methods, weights, sizes, shapes, method of operation, packaging, and power, temperature, and pressure ratings.

A third type of catalog is the counter or in-store catalog. This is used as a reference by store employees and customers at the point of sale.

A catalog is useful when you are selling a large number of products geared to one type of buyer. A software publisher with a library of 60 game cartridges would logically use a catalog aimed at buyers of computer and video games. In contrast, a programmer who designs customized software for a specific industry, such as transportation, would be better off with a brochure outlining the unique services offered.

6. Circular

A circular is a printed sheet used by retailers to announce sales and specials. The circular is usually printed in color on newspaper stock and in newspaper format. Circulars can be mailed, distributed door-to-door, inserted in newspapers, or made available at supermarket checkout counters, shopping malls, and other points of sale.

The focus of the circular is on generating immediate retail sales through price-off coupons, discounts, and other specials. The circular is a short-lived promotion piece that is used only as long as the sales goes on. After the sale the circular is discarded and a new one is written for the next promotion.

Who uses circulars? Supermarkets, drug stores, stereo and electronic equipment stores, department stores, and any other retailer with merchandise to move.

7. Data sheet

A product data sheet (also called a *specification sheet* or *spec sheet*) contains detailed facts and specifications about a product.

The data sheet is used at the end of the sales cycle. The prospect has responded to your ad, and your sales brochure has piqued his interest. Now, nearly ready to buy, the consumer has some questions that need to be answered. The data sheet is designed to provide those answers.

"The data sheet should answer all of the customer's questions," writes Joe Lane, president of J. J. Lane, Inc., in an article in *Sales & Marketing Management*. "If the information the customer needs to make the buying decision isn't there, the data sheet is worthless."

Data sheets are usually 8½″ × 11″ with copy on both sides. Longer data sheets can run four to six pages.

This is the place to put all your nuts-and-bolts information about the product, all the technical details you thought were too boring for your ad or general brochure. A data sheet describing the Halleyscope (a new telescope) includes descriptive information on the lens system, power range, camera adaptor, material of construction, tripod, zoom focus, carrying case, display case, filters, and shipping specifications.

8. Flier

A flier is an inexpensive piece of promotional literature with simple copy and line art printed on one side of an 8½″ × 11″ sheet of paper.

Fliers can be posted on community bulletin boards or distributed by hand. They provide an inexpensive way for local businesses to get their message across to people in the neighborhood.

In the past six months I've received fliers from such diverse businesses as a typing service, a pizza parlor, a Chinese restaurant, an exterminator, a locksmith, a music teacher, a handyman, a painter, a plumber, a limousine service, a taxi company, a computer dealer, and a hair salon.

Just about any business serving local residents can benefit from distributing a flier. It should state the name of the business, the product or service offered, and the store location, hours, and telephone number.

Fliers are not appropriate for expensive products or systems, large national companies, or products sold to upscale (wealthy and sophisticated) buyers. The reason is that fliers, being inexpensive to produce, tend to have a cheap look about them. A company worried about projecting a dignified or successful image would not want to use them.

9. Invoice stuffer

An invoice stuffer is a pamphlet or flier sent along with the consumer's monthly invoice. American Express is a heavy user of invoice stuffers, offering collectibles, clocks, pen sets, and other fine products by mail. My local cable TV company uses invoice stuffers to promote subscriptions to new channels and program services.

The great advantage of invoice stuffers is that they get a free ride in the mail because they're sent with invoices, statements, and other regularly mailed correspondence.

Of course, if you don't mail out monthly statements or bills, you can't take advantage of invoice stuffers on a large scale. However, you can still print up a batch of invoice stuffers and send them out whenever you do write a letter or mail a bill. Even a small volume can produce profitable returns.

10. Newsletter

A newsletter is a short, regularly published periodical sent to employees, customers, and prospects.

Newsletters do not generate immediate sales. Instead, they build your image and keep your name in front of the select group of people you mail it to over a long period of time.

Many organizations publish newsletters as promotional tools, but the reader expects a newsletter to contain real news. Therefore, your newsletter should be a blend of industry and company news, useful information, and sales pitch for your product or service. But be careful. If the product pitch is too blatant, or if it dominates the newsletter, readers will throw the newsletter away. The key to getting them to read and keep it is to publish information that is timely or helpful.

For a small to medium-sized company, a two- to four-page newsletter published four times a year (once per quarter) seems just about right.

11. Poster

Some companies take a full-page flier or ad, blow it up to poster size, and mail it in a cardboard tube to prospective customers.

Literature mailed this way almost always gets opened and read. After all, a 3-foot-long mailing tube is sure to stand out in a $9'' \times 13''$ "in" basket full of standard $4'' \times 9''$ white business envelopes. People are naturally curious, and so they will open the tube, unravel the poster, and read at least part of the copy.

Unfortunately, most people won't save your poster. People like to keep sales literature handy in a file folder, desk drawer, or three-ring binder, and the poster won't fit in any of these. It's far easier to throw the poster away than to try and find a place to keep it.

Most poster advertisers hope that the recipient will hang the poster on the office or study wall. The reality is that few people consider your advertising literature a work of art, and it is the rare poster that is attractive or interesting enough to be hung in the prospect's home or office. (Of course, those posters that do make it act as a daily reminder of a company and its sales pitch.)

One way to increase the poster's chances of getting taped to the wall is to enhance it with some useful information: a calendar, an inspirational message, a metric conversion table, a product selection guide.

Deciding Whether You Need Promotional Literature

Chances are you've already decided that you need a brochure or other kind of promotional literature. Otherwise, you wouldn't have bought this book. But I'll assume that a percentage of the people reading this haven't made that decision yet.

For those people, I've compiled the following list of some of the reasons why companies publish promotional literature. If any of the situations described below sounds somewhat like your own, then it's a safe bet that there's a brochure in your future.

■ **Your potential customers ask for it**

If people who walk into your office or call you on the phone constantly ask to see a brochure, that's reason enough to have one. It means that your prospects need more information before they're ready to buy. If you don't provide it, you may lose the sale. And if your competitors have literature and you don't, you're at a disadvantage. You must be ready to respond to that common request, "Can you send me a brochure?"

■ **Your salespeople ask for it**

Salespeople are in the best position to know what support they need from the home office in order to make the sale. And helping them to make the sale is a major function of promotional literature. So if your salespeople make repeated requests for you to supply them with printed materials, it will probably be profitable for you to do so.

■ **You sell to business and industry**

As I mentioned earlier, Thomas Publishing Company reports that 90 percent of industrial buyers insist on seeing printed literature before they buy. Having a brochure is a must for anyone selling products and services to business, industry, and professionals.

■ **You sell through agents**

Sales reps, distributors, and other agents who carry your product line expect you to support their selling efforts with first-class brochures, case history bulletins, data sheets, and other literature. It is just about impossible to convince a middleman to take on your line if you have no literature.

These distributors and reps rarely produce their own literature. They prefer to take your brochure and imprint it with their logo and address.

■ **You run ads, send out press releases, or use telemarketing to generate leads**

Even a modest advertising and publicity campaign can generate hundreds or thousands of inquiries by mail and phone. It is impossible to answer all of these inquiries with a personal phone call, visit, or letter.

Mass-produced sales literature is the answer. Mailing a brochure and form letter is the only way to efficiently and economically answer the queries generated by advertising and publicity.

■ **You use direct mail to generate leads**

The most effective way to generate response to a sales letter is to offer a free sales brochure or informative booklet to readers who phone or mail the reply card. Naturally, if you make such an offer, you must have literature on hand to fulfill the requests.

■ **Your product is a "considered purchase"**

A *considered purchase* is a buying decision that the buyer has spent some time thinking about. Most major buying decisions are considered purchases, such as the decision to buy a car, home, refrigerator, microwave oven, stock, sprinkler system, computer, typewriter, telephone system, encyclopedia, photocopier, or college education.

When the customer takes time to make a decision, any information that helps to make a wise choice will be eagerly accepted. A brochure provides this information and helps sway the customer by presenting the advantages and highlights of your product.

When making an impulse purchase, without taking the time to mull over the advantages and drawbacks of a product, the customer probably won't want to bother reading literature and so a brochure is not required. Record albums, paperback novels, ice cream cones, fast foods, greeting cards, ballpoint pens, and umbrellas (especially on a rainy day!) are all impulse items, as is virtually every type of packaged good. (Packaged goods are items sold off the shelf at supermarkets and drug stores. They include toothpaste, shampoo, bathroom tissue, deodorant, coffee, and canned foods.)

■ **Your product or service has tangible features and benefits**

Products whose function, construction, and benefits can be described in words and pictures are particularly well suited to be the subject of a sales brochure. For example, you could write thousands of words describing the virtues of a new car, furnace, or home-study course.

There are many other products that don't have tangible features, and there is very little to say about these products. Take soda pop, for example. You can say that it tastes good and is refreshing, but that's about it. Even worse, every other soda pop can make these claims. So you'd have a hard time writing a brochure on the subject. Fortunately, most of the products in this category are impulse items, so there's really no need to produce a brochure.

■ Your business is new and you want people to know about it

A corporate brochure can go a long way toward educating people about a new business venture. The more brochures you distribute, the more people there are who know of your existence.

Also, most new businesses have a credibility problem. People are reluctant to deal with the new business because they have never heard of it. They want proof that the company is real and not some fly-by-night operation. A corporate brochure can provide that proof.

■ Your company is growing and you want people to understand it

As companies grow they become more complex. What was a simple business is now a multinational corporation with many products, many offices, many divisions, and many different groups of customers. A company brochure helps give people a clear picture of the corporation and its mission.

■ You want to increase sales

Literature can be an effective promotional tool for generating leads, increasing sales, gaining new members, raising funds, bringing in votes, or getting support for your project or idea. Unlike print ads, where space is limited, or TV commercials, where time is short, brochures give you as much space as you need to make your sales pitch.

What's more, brochures allow you to get your message across to those people you can't contact by phone or personal visit. A friend of mine calls his brochures "silent salesmen," because every brochure sitting in a person's file or desk drawer may, at any time, be pulled from the file or drawer and turned into a sale. If you want to boost sales, create a persuasive piece of sales literature and get it into the hands of as many of your prospective customers as you can.

■ **You want to build an image**

The look, feel, and tone of your promotional literature has much to do with the way the public perceives you. Do you want to be known as aggressive or laid back? Dynamic or dignified? Small and smart or large and established? Promotional literature can show the public the image you want to project.

■ **You simply want a brochure**

A perfectly valid reason for producing a brochure is that you want one. I know many entrepreneurs who claim they didn't feel they were running real companies until they published their brochures. A brochure can be a boost to your own morale as well as the morale of your partners and employees. A brochure can also solidify the direction and purpose of a company, perhaps because people take things more seriously when they see these things in print.

CHAPTER TWO

GETTING STARTED: PLANNING, SCHEDULING, BUDGETING

This chapter addresses considerations that are basic to creating promotional literature whether you're planning a single brochure or a whole series of pieces.

Setting Your Objective

Your objective might be to:

- Provide product information to customers
- Educate new prospects
- Build a corporate image
- Establish credibility for your firm or product
- Sell the product directly through the mail
- Help salespeople get appointments
- Help salespeople make presentations
- Help close the sale
- Support dealers, distributors, and sales reps
- Add value to the product
- Enhance the effectiveness of direct-mail packages
- Leave a reminder with customers
- Respond to inquiries
- Hand something out at trade shows, fairs, conventions
- Display at point of purchase
- Disseminate news about the company and its products
- Announce new products and product improvements
- Train and educate new managers, engineers, and salespeople

- Recruit new employees
- Provide useful information to the public
- Generate new business leads
- Qualify to be on a customer's approved-vendors list

Whether it's intended to cause the reader to take some action or to change her or his understanding of or attitude toward you and your product, your brochure should be created for a specific purpose. If after reading the brochure the reader remains unchanged or isn't moved to take action, you've failed.

Know the objective of your brochure. Be able to state it in a brief sentence or two. If you can't think of a reason for publishing the brochure, maybe it doesn't need to be published.

Choosing an Appropriate Format

The next step is to decide exactly what type of printed literature you need. Figure 2.1 provides a selection guide you can use to choose the format that's right for your application.

Figure 2.1   Eleven types of literature you can use to promote your company, product, or service.

Use this	To
Annual report	• Build your image • Disclose financial information • Communicate with shareholders, investors, and the financial community • Tell your corporate story to customers, employees, and the business community • Provide a quick overview of your business to potential customers, outside vendors, and the press • Sell stock • Impress vendors and other companies you deal with • Recruit new employees
Booklet	• Provide useful information • Answer questions frequently asked by customers and prospects

(Continued)

Figure 2.1   Continued.

Use this	To
	■ Generate more sales leads (by offering the booklet in advertising or direct mail) ■ Teach customers to be informed consumers of your type of product
Brochure	■ Promote any product, service, or program ■ Help salespeople get appointments ■ Help salespeople close sales ■ Answer inquiries ■ Provide product information to customers and prospects ■ Establish your product in the marketplace
Case history	■ Tell prospects and customers about the successful performance of your product or service ■ Overcome skepticism ■ Describe uses of the product in special applications ■ Get testimonials for use in advertising, publicity, and other promotions ■ Show a customer how to solve her or his problem
Catalog	■ Sell an entire product line instead of just a single product ■ Sell products by mail ■ Help buyers find and select the products they need ■ Serve as a single source for all the customer's needs
Circular	■ Increase retail sales ■ Promote Christmas sales and other special events ■ Clear your warehouse of dead merchandise through discounts and other special deals ■ Put coupons into the hands of shoppers
Data sheet	■ Answer buyers' questions ■ Help salespeople close the sale ■ Satisfy the information needs of dealers, manufacturers' representatives, purchasing agents, and others

Figure 2.1   Continued.

Flier
- Promote your business on a local level
- Sell a product or service
- Get your name around
- Announce an event

Invoice stuffer
- Reinforce a sales message
- Provide useful information to customers
- Announce sales and specials
- Sell products and supplies by mail
- Communicate with employees and customers

Newsletter
- Communicate with employees, customers, and prospects
- Keep your name before customers and prospects
- Build the buyer's trust in your organization over a long period of time
- Supplement your other promotional efforts
- Get more sales leads (by asking people to request a free subscription to your newsletter)
- Disseminate news and late-breaking product information and updates
- Advise your customers of new applications, new accessories, new policies, new products

Poster
- Have your message stand out from the crowd
- Create some excitement about your product
- Get your name in front of the buyer
- Increase repeat business

Determining the Subject of the Brochure

Before you can write a brochure, you have to know what you want to write about. This means being able to specify the subject of the brochure, the scope of information you want to include, and the overall theme or story you want to tell. It also means knowing what *shouldn't* be included.

Is the brochure about a single product? Two products? A product line? A particular application of a product?

What information should be included? What should be excluded? Don't just guess; have a reason for including or excluding a particular fact.

Does the brochure merely present a set of facts or does it tell a story? If it does tell a story, what should that story be? The theme dictates how you arrange and organize the copy.

Do you have all the facts? Do you know all you need to about your product, your market, and your industry? Or is research required to fill in missing facts? If you're missing vital information, start collecting it *now*; otherwise, it may hold you up later on.

When you are sure of your subject, everything else falls neatly into place. When you don't know what you're selling, chaos and confusion plague the production process every step of the way.

It is not enough simply to list all the facts and features of your product and hope that is what the reader is looking for. You have to describe the *benefits* of the product, the reasons why the reader would want to buy it. And you've got to highlight these benefits in your brochure.

Market-research questionnaires, focus groups, and surveys can all be used to find out which product benefits and features your customers care most about. An informal telephone survey of half a dozen or so customers and potential customers can reveal volumes about your product, how it is perceived in the marketplace, and what your customers really are looking for.

Take a look at your competitors' brochures. See how they present themselves and their products. What sales appeals are highlighted? Which are omitted? Perhaps you can emphasize a benefit that your competitors neglected to stress, and win customers that way.

Don't forget to factor in your other promotional efforts. Will you have more than one brochure? If so, you must determine where each piece fits in to your sales cycle. You might have a small pamphlet for answering initial inquiries, a more detailed sales brochure used by your salespeople, and data sheets to close the sale. Each brochure should move the reader one step closer to placing an order.

Your brochures should complement your other promotional efforts: print advertising, direct mail, trade show displays, and publicity. There should be a common graphic look to all your marketing materials, and all the pieces should work in harmony to achieve a common sales goal (See Figure 2.2). A brochure used to answer inquiries, for example, should expand upon the themes and answer the questions raised in the print ad. And the design of product manuals and instruction sheets should match the product's packaging.

Figure 2.2   All elements in this family of literature—brochure, fact sheets, letterhead, and business cards—use the same typeface, logo, and paper stock to ensure a consistent look.

Bob Bly

Copywriter/Consultant/Seminar Leader

22 East Quackenbush Avenue, 3rd floor
Dumont, NJ 07628
Phone (201) 385-1220 • Fax (201) 385-1138

Marketing Communications Planning, Strategy, Consultation, and Copy

In today's economy, it pays to make every marketing communication count. But do yours?

From time to time, you've probably felt the need for help in planning, creating, and implementing effective direct mail, advertising, and public relations programs. For example, maybe you need advice and assistance in:

- Converting more leads to sales
- Generating more inquiries from print advertising
- Determining which vertical industries or narrow target markets to pursue
- Producing effective sales brochures, catologs, case histories, and other marketing literature
- Writing and placing press releases, feature stories, and other publicity materials
- Creating response-getting direct mail offers, packages, and campaigns
- Designing, writing, and producing a company newsletter
- Or any of dozens of other marketing problems.

Maybe you've felt that the usual sources of assistance—freelancers, advertising agencies, and PR firms—were not focused on solving your particular problems, lacked the specific knowledge you require, didn't understand your product or service, charged unreasonable prices, or were not interested in your project because they wanted all your business.

Or maybe you just want some occasional guidance and assistance, and prefer to handle most of your marketing communications in-house.

Now there's a service designed especially to help you—

Marketing Communications Planning, Strategy, and Consultation

From Bob Bly—Copywriter/Consultant/Seminar Leader

Here are some questions prospective clients typically ask me—and the answers:

What is the Marketing Communications Planning, Strategy, and Consultation Service? This is a service which assists small and medium-size firms in planning, creating, and implementing effective advertising, marketing, direct mail, publicity, and promotional programs. I act as your ongoing adviser, answering your questions, making recommendations, and providing whatever help you need to market and promote your product or service successfully.

How does it work? My service is flexible and available to you on whatever basis meets your needs. You can hire me by the project, by the day, by the hour, or on a flexible retainer basis. While I am happy to use our time in any way you like, I will always advise you on how I think you will get the best results for your money.

- over -

(Continued)

Figure 2.2   Continued.

Bob Bly
Copywriter/Consultant/Seminar Leader

22 East Quackenbush Avenue
3rd floor
Dumont, NJ 07628
Phone (201) 385-1220
Fax (201) 385-1138

Thanks for your interest
In my copywriting services…

Now, maybe you asked for this information kit out of curiosity. Some folks do—especially those who never hired a freelance copywriter before.

But, more likely, you need a good business-to-business copy-writer—someone who combines writing skill and sales ability with technical know-how and product knowledge.

Whatever your reason for calling or writing, you want to know more about a writer before you hire him. If we were sitting face-to-face, chatting in your office, you'd ask me questions. Let me try to answer a few of those questions right here.

"WHAT ARE YOUR QUALIFICATIONS AS A COPYWRITER?"

As a freelancer, I've written copy for over 100 agencies and advertisers. And, I'm the author of 17 books including THE COPY-WRITER'S HANDBOOK (Dodd, Mead), CREATE THE PERFECT SALES PIECE (John Wiley), and DIRECT MAIL PROFITS: HOW TO GET MORE LEADS AND SALES BY MAIL (Asher-Gallant Press).

In addition, I write a monthly column on copywriting for Direct Marketing magazine. I also teach copywriting at New York University.

Before becoming a freelancer, I was advertising manager for Koch Engineering (an industrial manufacturer) and a staff writer for Westinghouse. The attached material will give you the full story.

"DO YOU HAVE A TECHNICAL BACKGROUND?"

I have a Bachelor's degree in engineering from the University of Rochester. And, 95 percent of the work I do is in industrial, high-tech, business-to-business, and direct response.

I've written copy in computers, chemicals, pulp and paper, mining, construction, electronics, engineering, pollution control, industrial equipment, marine products, software, banking, financial services, health care, publishing, seminars, training, telecommunications, consulting, corporate, and many other areas. In the personal computer field, for example, I'm the author of five computer books including A DICTIONARY OF COMPUTER WORDS, published by Dell/Banbury.

Most important to you, I'm a business-to-business, direct-response copy specialist. Writing business-to-business copy isn't something I do to pass the time between TV commercials. Rather, it's

(over, please...)

Figure 2.2   Continued.

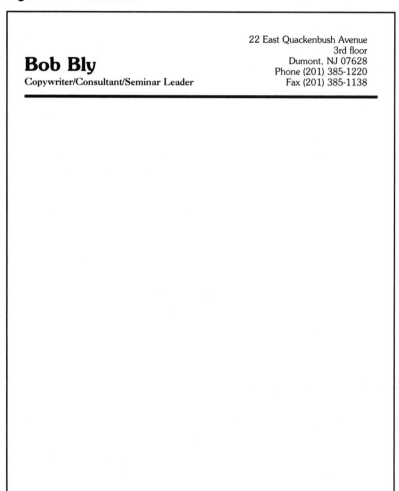

Targeting Your Audience

With a promotion piece, you want to be sure of a receptive audience, and so you tailor your promotion to your audience. That way, you have a better chance of getting your message across. If you write in a vacuum, without thinking about who your reader is and what he or she wants to know, you're destined for failure.

"Your audience determines the design and diction of your piece," says Elizabeth Morse-Cluley, director of publications at Mercy College. "For example, a tour map for children should be 'bright' and simple in form and content; an annual report should be sophisticated and detailed in form and content."

Of course, you can't go out and interview all your prospects to find out what they like or dislike, what they believe in and what they're against. But you can learn much from the general characteristics of your target audience. For consumer marketing, these characteristics include age, geographic location, income, sex, family status, education, wealth, ethnic background, and religion.

For brochures aimed at business prospects, key characteristics you want to know about your audience include occupation, size of company, job title and responsibilities, and industry.

Creating the Right Image

Regardless of whether image-building is its primary goal, your brochure conveys an image, too—an image of your organization.

By consciously controlling the tone, look, and feel of your brochure, you can create the image you want to convey. Some of the elements that affect the image your literature portrays include paper stock, color, copy tone and style, quality of photos and illustrations, size, number of pages, typography, design, and page layout.

Start collecting your competitors' brochures and the brochures of non-competing firms that offer products or services similar to yours. Study this competitor literature to find ideas you can use as well as ways you can differentiate yourself from the pack.

Determining Costs and Setting a Budget

Here is a list of the expenses involved in producing promotional literature along with the suppliers who handle each particular phase of the job:

Task	Vendor	Cost ($)
Text	Writer	_____
Photography	Photographer or stock photo house	_____
Artwork	Graphic designer or illustrator	_____
Typography	Type house, graphic designer, or desktop publishing service	_____
Design	Graphic designer, art studio, or desktop publishing service	_____
Mechanical	Graphic designer, paste-up artist, art studio, or desktop publishing service	_____
Printing	Printer	_____
	TOTAL COST: $	_____

To ensure that you pay a fair price, you should get bids from three different suppliers for each phase of the job. To ensure that you get an accurate quotation, you must give each supplier complete specifications for the job.

The writer needs to know approximate word count, what source material you can supply, and whether any research or travel is involved. The graphic designer or art studio needs to know, as precisely as possible, the format of the piece: number of words, number and size of pages, number and type of visuals (photos, drawings, etc.), how many colors will be used, and the degree of design sophistication you're looking for (plain, fancy, or in-between).

The more accurate and precise your specifications, the more accurate the price quotations will be. If you're vague, the vendors will have to make their best guess, and their uncertainty will be reflected in a higher price. In addition, the price can change substantially if you change the specifications once the job is underway.

Once you add up price quotations from the various vendors, you may be shocked to find that producing the brochure costs much more than you thought it would. This is likely to happen if you haven't had much recent experience hiring writers, photographers, artists, and other professionals. Their services can mean the difference between a successful brochure and a poor one, but these services are not cheap.

Does this mean you can't afford to produce a brochure? Of course not! You can cut corners and do away with some luxury items (such as shooting a photo of your Bermuda plant on location) and still end up with a first-class piece.

Advances in computer technology and desktop publishing have made many aspects of brochure production less costly; for example, typesetting using desktop publishing is less than half the cost of using conventional type-setting houses. With your own desktop publishing system, you can even do the typesetting, page layout, and design work yourself, from initial concept to printing a camera-ready proof for the printer.

Determining the Brochure's Length and Size

Will your brochure be a slim-jim or full size? Two pages or twenty-four? You need to make an educated guess as to the number of words of text, the number and type of visuals, the number and size of pages, and the number of colors to give to your vendors so they can provide accurate, fair estimates for cost.

Make your rough estimate of word count as follows: When you type the copy you'll use double-spacing (for easy editing): a double-spaced typewritten sheet contains about 250 words. Make a list of the topics you plan to cover in the brochure. Then guess how many pages will have to be written to cover the topic adequately. If you're not sure, set a range (three to four pages, for example). Add up the page count for all the sections, multiply the total by 250, and you have your rough word count for estimating typography and writer's fees.

Estimating the number and type of visuals is a little easier. You simply make a list of all the subjects that you want to visualize, then assign the type of treatment most appropriate to each (new photo, existing photo, stock photo, fine art, line drawing, graph, table, etc.). You'll have to balance your ideas and personal preferences with what can actually be done within your budget guidelines.

Page size depends on how you want to present the information and how the brochure is to be used. If your brochure consists of many short, separate sections, a smaller page size may be most appropriate. If the brochure consists of a small number of lengthy sections illustrated with elaborate graphs and diagrams, the standard 8½″ × 11″ page is best.

For a brochure that will be used in direct mail, the smaller size may be more economical in terms of envelopes and postage. But the small brochure can get lost in a file folder or binder, whereas the larger brochure won't. An oversized brochure (larger than 11 inches high) may grab attention when received but is likely to be discarded because it won't fit in a standard file folder or cabinet.

Once you've selected the page size, the number of pages depends on the content and design. The more copy and visuals you have, the longer the brochure. However, a given brochure can have few pages if a lot of copy and artwork is crammed onto each page. Or it can be many pages long if the designer leaves a lot of "white space" and places a minimum of art and copy on each page. The size of the type also helps determine the number of pages.

To give you a rough idea of what is typical for a brochure with full size (7″ × 10″ or 8½″ × 11″) pages, the average brochure, with a column or so of text and a couple of photos, contains from 250 to 400 words per page.

A brochure with very dense copy in two or three columns (similar to a full-page article in a magazine) can have as many as 500 to 600 words per page.

A brochure or other literature using sparse text with a lot of light space and visuals, such as a catalog or corporate capabilities piece, might have only 200 or so words per page.

Whether to use color is another decision you'll make early on. The most inexpensive brochures are printed in one color. This is usually black on white, but it doesn't have to be. Sometimes you can create an expensive-looking effect by printing in colored ink on a colored stock, such as maroon ink on gray paper or dark brown ink on off-white or beige stock.

A second color can highlight portions of text, headlines, and visuals. It gives the designer another element to work with, and adds only about 15 to 20 percent to the cost of printing.

Brochures with reproductions of color photos are called *full-color* brochures. Full-color printing is the most expensive, and each color photo you add will boost production costs by at least several hundred dollars.

The choice of paper stock also has a great effect on printing costs. You won't make the final selection until you're sitting down with printers to get printing bids, but now is the time to make some initial decisions: Do you want glossy or nonglossy stock? Heavy or lightweight paper? A smooth stock or a paper with body, feel, and texture? Do you want the cover printed in a heavier stock than the inside pages? Will you use white or colored paper?

If you find it hard to describe what you want in words or sketches, get some paper, tape, and scissors and make a crude mock-up of the piece. Such a mock-up is known as a *dummy*. The dummy gives people an idea of the size, format, fold, look, and weight of the finished piece.

Another way of communicating your ideas on layout and format is to find a similar brochure published by another organization and show it to your artist or printer. I keep a thick file folder that contains all printed pieces of literature that catch my eye. When I want to describe a particular look, style, typeface, paper stock, or graphic technique to someone, I can usually find a sample of what I want in this file. You might want to do the same.

Don't worry about making the wrong choice or whether you have bad taste. Remember that you're not locked in to a particular format until the job goes to the printer, and your designer may suggest alternatives to what you originally selected. But you should try to decide on the basic format now so you'll be better able to describe to others the look you want to achieve.

Scheduling

How long should it take to produce a brochure?

It depends. You can write, design, and print a simple flier in a week, whereas an annual report can take three or four months to complete.

My observation is: the more time, the better. I'd rather extend the deadline and get it right than do a rush job that is less than perfect. After all, producing literature is expensive, and you'll have to live with most pieces a long time.

Jane Maas, a senior officer at the Wells, Rich, Greene advertising agency, says that you should allow 120 days from the start of writing and design to delivery of the finished literature from the printer. My experience has proven that to be a good guideline for scheduling.

That time frame is for a major piece with detailed copy, professional graphic design, original photography and illustration, and color printing. For a simple flier or circular, a desktop publishing service might be able to give you camera-ready proofs in just a couple of days, and the local print shop can run off hundreds or thousands of copies in just a few days more.

Each phase of each project will take a different amount of time to complete. Sketching a few simple line drawings for a small pamphlet may take an artist only a few hours; illustrating a large brochure on a complicated medical procedure might involve several weeks of work.

To help you plan, I've listed the stages of brochure production in the left-hand column below. The middle column indicates how many days the task normally takes to complete on a "major" brochure project. Right now, use the form below as a guide; when you are further along, you can fill in the blanks in the third column. To do so, you'll have to get estimates from the writer, artist, typesetter, and printer to find out the time each phase of your project will take.

Task	Days to complete (typical project)	Days to complete (your project)
Research and writing	10	_____
Copy review	5	_____
Copy rewrite	5	_____
Design	10	_____
Design review	5	_____
Design revision	5	_____
Typesetting	3	_____
Photography	10	_____
Illustration	10	_____
Mechanicals	5	_____
Printing (add 15 days for four-color)	10	_____
Delays, mistakes	5	_____
TOTAL DAYS:	78	_____

On some projects, you'll be uncertain as to the exact content and appearance of the finished piece, and you will have to finish one phase of the project before you go on to the next. (For example, you can't take photos until the design is approved and you know what visuals you want.) If that's the case, you can follow the sequence of steps as they're listed above: copy, design, typesetting, art and photography, paste-up, and printing.

According to my schedule, that should take 78 days. If your suppliers work fast, you can cut down on the time. But if there are problems—the photos don't come out, there are mistakes in the type, the copywriter does a bad job—they can easily add a month to the job. That's why Jane Maas's 120-day rule of thumb is a good one.

However, if you've carefully followed and analyzed the first nine key planning points presented in this chapter, you may have a clear enough description of the finished piece to combine steps and save time. If, for example, you know the format and the visuals you want, you can write the copy and do the design, illustration, and photography all at once. After that, you would set type, paste up the mechanical (camera-ready copy), and print the brochure.

By combining steps, you can cut the time required to 43 days—an example of how some planning can save you time.

To Sum It All Up

I know we've covered a lot of ground in this chapter. To help you put it all together, I've included a literature specification sheet, shown in Figure 2.3. This form provides a handy way of collecting the information discussed throughout this chapter.

Make copies of the form and keep them handy. When you're contemplating your next project, fill out the specification sheet as completely as possible. Then circulate copies of the completed sheet to vendors and company personnel involved in the project. Vendors can use the information to provide accurate price quotations and your people can see at a glance the project you've planned.

Figure 2.3   Literature Specification Sheet.

1. Objectives of the literature (check all that are appropriate):
   (   ) Provide product information to customers
   (   ) Educate new prospects
   (   ) Build corporate image
   (   ) Establish credibility of your organization or product
   (   ) Sell the product direct through the mail
   (   ) Help salespeople get appointments
   (   ) Help salespeople make presentations
   (   ) Help close the sale
   (   ) Support dealers, distributors, and sales representatives
   (   ) Add value to the product
   (   ) Enhance the effectiveness of direct-mail promotions
   (   ) Leave with customers as a reminder
   (   ) Respond to inquiries
   (   ) Hand out at trade shows, fairs, conventions
   (   ) Display at point of purchase
   (   ) Serve as reference material for employees, vendors, the press
   (   ) Disseminate news
   (   ) Announce new products and product improvements
   (   ) Highlight new applications for existing products
   (   ) Train and educate new employees
   (   ) Recruit new employees
   (   ) Provide useful information to the public
   (   ) Generate new business leads
   (   ) Qualify your company to be on a customer's approved-vendor list
   (   ) Other (describe): _____

   _____

2. The type of literature needed (check one):
   (   ) annual report (   ) booklet   (   ) brochure
   (   ) case history   (   ) catalog   (   ) circular   (   ) data sheet
   (   ) flier (   ) invoice stuffer   (   ) newsletter   (   ) poster
   (   ) other (describe): _____

(Continued)

Figure 2.3　Continued.

3. The subject
   a.　What is the subject matter of the literature (describe the product, service, program, organization, and so forth)?

   b.　What is the theme, the central message (if any)?

   c.　What supporting information is to be included (price, reliability,
   efficiency, performance, quality, test results, testimonials, technical specifications, and so forth)?

   d.　What is the source of this information (where can the writer get
   the necessary background material?

   e.　What facts are missing? What research is required (if any)?

4. Who is the audience?
   a.　Geographic location _____
   b.　Income level _____
   c.　Family status (married/single) _____
   d.　Industry _____
   e.　Job title/function _____
   f.　Education _____
   g.　Politics _____
   h.　Religion/ethnic background _____
   i.　Age _____

Figure 2.3   Continued.

j.   Concerns (reasons why they might be interested in the subject matter of the literature):

_____

_____

k.   General description of the target audience (in your own words):

_____

5. Sales appeals
   a.   What is the key sales appeal of the product?

   b.   What are the supporting or secondary sales points?

6. What image do you want the literature to convey to the reader?

7. Environment
   a.   What image and sales appeals do competitors' brochures stress?

Competitor	Image	Key sales appeal
_____	_____	_____
_____	_____	_____
_____	_____	_____
_____	_____	_____
_____	_____	_____

   b.   How does the brochure fit into your sales cycle (check all that apply)?
   ( ) Generate leads
   ( ) Answer initial inquiries
   ( ) Provide more detailed information to qualified buyers
   ( ) Establish confidence in company and its product
   ( ) Provide detailed product information
   ( ) Answer questions frequently asked by prospects

(Continued)

Figure 2.3   Continued.

( ) Provide support for salespeople during presentations
( ) Reinforce sales message for prospects ready to buy
( ) Close the sale
( ) Other (describe):

8. Budget (What will it cost to produce?)

Task	Cost ($)
Copywriting	_____
Photography	_____
Artwork	_____
Typography	_____
Design	_____
Mechanicals	_____
Printing	_____
Total:	$ _____

Number of copies to be printed: _____

9. Format
   a.   Approximate number of words _____
   b.   Number of color photos _____
   c.   Number of black-and-white photos _____
   d.   Number and type of illustrations and other visuals (describe):

   e.   Number of pages _____
   f.   Page size _____
   g.   Method of folding or binding (describe):
   h.   Number of colors used in printing _____
   i.   Color scheme of brochure (describe) _____

   j.   Type of paper (weight, finish, texture, color) _____

Figure 2.3 Continued.

10. Schedule (How long will it take to complete?)

Task	Number of days to complete
Copy	_____
Copy review	_____
Copy rewrite	_____
Design	_____
Design review	_____
Design revision	_____
Typesetting	_____
Photography	_____
Illustration	_____
Mechanicals	_____
Printing	_____
Delays, mistakes	_____
Total:	_____

CHAPTER THREE

PEOPLE WHO CAN HELP YOU (AND WHERE TO FIND THEM)

Can you do the brochure yourself? Or do you need help?

It *is* possible to handle the job yourself (except for the printing, of course). You can write the copy, take the photos, use *clip art* (stock illustrations) or create your own visuals, do the design and layout on your Macintosh or other personal computer using desktop publishing software, and produce a camera-ready mechanical with 300 dpi (dots per inch) resolution using a laser printer.

If you're producing a simple flier or brochure, you can even run off copies one at a time on your laser printer. But using your printer as a press puts wear and tear on it. For substantial quantities—200 copies or more—you're better off having copies run off at a local quick-print shop. It's relatively fast, and it's inexpensive if the brochure does not have too many pages.

Why, then, would you want to hire a writer, photographer, artist, or illustrator? For two reasons: quality and time.

Some business people do have a talent for art, photography, or copy. If you can write better than the ad agency copywriter, or take photos of professional quality, you may want to do these tasks yourself and save some money.

On the other hand, time is money, and your time is precious. Even if, thanks to desktop publishing, you feel you can design page layouts as well as or better than your ad agency art director, is designing brochures and picking out fonts really how you should be spending your time? Or should you concentrate on your core business activity of managing, planning, and running a company (or whatever) and leave the nuts-and-bolts details to hired professionals?

Should you produce your own brochure? I'm not saying that you should never tackle brochure work. If you simply can't afford professional help, or if you have the artistic and mechanical skills and the right computer equipment, you may be able to save money by doing much of the job yourself.

However, most of us aren't writers, artists, photographers, illustrators, and designers all rolled into one. So we look to outside professionals to help us with these tasks.

How important is the brochure to you? What level of quality do you desire? For most of us, our brochure is like a company salesperson on paper. Just as you wouldn't send a salesperson out in a cheap suit with a stained necktie, you don't really want to send out a brochure that makes you look cheap and poor.

Above all, you want to avoid poor quality and amateurish work. If you don't have the money to hire a professional photographer, and neither you nor anyone you know can take professional-quality photos, either don't use photos or try to get the photos you need from another source, such as a stock photo house, a book, a magazine, or another organization (many manufacturers provide free product photos to their distributors for use in circulars, local advertising, and other promotions).

If there isn't an inexpensive source for the photo you need, it's better to omit photos than to use the fuzzy shots taken by Uncle Joe. Perhaps simpler, less expensive spot drawings will do just as well. Or maybe the copy says it all, and you don't even need a visual. Often you'll find that the fancy photography, artwork, design, or typography you want but can't afford isn't really necessary in the first place.

Some projects do require more sophisticated design and production, and that's where the services of professionals are especially needed. This chapter will teach you how to find, choose, and work with various advertising professionals. Chapters 4–9 have more of a do-it-yourself focus.

Let's start by introducing all the people and organizations you might call on for help: advertising agencies, public relations firms, creative boutiques, marketing communications firms, design studios, copywriters, graphic artists, desktop publishing services, service bureaus, photographers, illustrators, typographers, and printers.

Advertising Agencies

The main advantage of using an advertising agency is that it will handle the entire job for you, from strategy and concept to copywriting and design to production and printing. The ad agency will assign an account executive to act as liaison between you and the various departments of the agency. You'll be spared having to coordinate the work of a writer, artist, photographer, printer, and other outside suppliers; the agency will do it all.

The disadvantage is that you'll pay a premium for this extra service. So you have to decide: Are you willing to pay to have someone else take over much of the burden of the job? Or do you want to save money by hiring a team of independent specialists (writer, designer, printer) and supervising the project yourself?

Another advantage of advertising agencies is that they're set up for handling coordinated campaigns to provide literature, advertising, publicity, and promotion. They can also act as advertising consultants, helping you to formulate a marketing plan and set your advertising strategy. So if you're planning a program with many pieces of sales literature and other promotions, an ad agency can orchestrate it for you and increase its effectiveness.

On the other hand, most advertising agencies shy away from one-shot projects. They prefer to work with clients on an ongoing basis. So if you're planning to produce only a single brochure or catalog, you'll have a hard time finding an ad agency willing to take on such a small amount of work. Even small advertising agencies expect a client to spend a minimum of about $50,000 a year on advertising and promotion. If your budget is less, an ad agency probably isn't for you.

Public Relations Firms

Public relations firms (PR) are specialists at getting free coverage for their clients in newspapers and magazines and on radio and TV. A public relations firm representing a bank, for example, might arrange to have the bank president interviewed on the evening news or get the press to cover the grand opening of a new branch.

Today many public relations firms produce promotional literature as an added service for their clients. The literature is used as handouts at press conferences and other special events or to answer inquiries generated by press coverage of an organization or its products.

Like advertising agencies, public relations firms handle the entire job for you, from initial idea to finished printed piece. However, most public relations firms require a monthly retainer from their clients, whereas most ad agencies do not. The minimum monthly retainer is usually $1,000, which comes to $12,000 a year. This means that a small organization without the budget to hire an ad agency can still afford the services of a PR firm, but you must pay the retainer fee even if you have no work for your PR firm that month.

Also, although many PR firms are quite skilled in literature production, their primary business is publicity, not brochures. If you hire a PR firm to handle your publicity, it might make sense to have that company do your literature as well. But if you need only literature and have no ongoing public relations campaign, you'll be better off using one of the other suppliers described below.

Design Studios

A design studio provides design and production for printed material. It designs the layout and look of the piece, then prepares a camera-ready mechanical for reproduction at the printer. Today many brochures are not reproduced from traditional mechanicals but are sent directly from the design studio to the printer either as camera-ready film from which a printing plate can be made or on computer disk.

Unlike an advertising agency, which handles all phases of the job and supervises every activity from start to finish, most design studios provide design services only. The majority of design studios do not write copy, create marketing plans, or do market research.

Let's say you already have good photos on file, can write the brochure yourself, and want to save money by going to the printer directly and eliminating the middleman. All you need is someone to do the layout and paste-up. A design studio may be the perfect solution for you.

These days many design studios are expanding their services to include copy, market research, and photography. But they rarely have writers, photographers, and researchers on staff. If they offer to handle the copy for you, it's likely they will go out and hire a free-lance writer.

Marketing Communications Companies

Marketing communications firms are similar to ad agencies but they usually do not handle media buying. A marketing communications firm usually consists of a writer and a graphic artist, and perhaps an account executive, all of whom probably left big ad agencies and teamed up to run their own small company.

These companies typically focus on sales promotion, direct mail, catalogs, brochures, and other collateral material. They can often provide the same quality and degree of service on sales brochure projects at less cost than an ad agency. And, they are perfectly happy to work on a project rather than contract or retainer basis.

Free-Lancers

Ad agencies and PR firms offer a completely integrated service: a single source for all phases of brochure production. Design studios and marketing communications companies offer some but not all services. At the other end are free-lancers, each handling one specific task: copywriting, illustration, photography, or design.

One advantage of using individual free-lancers instead of a single-source supplier is that free-lancers are available for small projects and one-time assignments. They work and get paid only when you need them. Agencies look for long-term commitment and shy away from one-shot projects.

Using free-lancers also gives you access to a diverse pool of talent and thus to a broader range of skills and ideas. You can select the specialist who is just right for the job, and work with her or him directly, eliminating the agency as the middleman. The fee is usually lower, because there is no mark-up on the free-lancer's services by an ad agency or PR firm.

A disadvantage is that the free-lancer who is only called in occasionally does not gain as much in-depth knowledge about your product and your business as do agencies and staff employees. Every time you work with a new free-lancer you have to brief her or him from scratch. And that can be time-consuming.

Copywriters

A *copywriter* is a person who writes copy—the text of advertising and promotional materials.

There are several ways to locate free-lance copywriters. One is word-of-mouth; ask business associates to recommend a writer. Another method is to run a help-wanted classified ad in your local paper using the headline "Free-lance writers wanted." You can also find free-lance copywriters listed in the Yellow Pages (under "writer," "copywriter," or "advertising services") and in the industry directories listed at the end of this chapter. Many copywriters also advertise their services in such advertising journals as *Adweek*, *Advertising Age*, and *Direct Marketing*.

What will you pay for copy? As free-lance copywriter Sig Rosenblum observes, "Fees are all over the lot." Of course, the more experienced the writer, the higher the charge.

At the bottom of the scale, some junior writers in rural locations charge as little as $20 to $35 an hour. Such a person can write competently enough to handle simple fliers and announcements but may lack the copywriting skill and product knowledge needed to tackle more complex tasks.

In the middle are generalists: copywriters who take on any assignment but have no particular specialty. These writers can produce good copy, but, because they have minimal background in your industry, they probably need a lot of help understanding your product and your marketing strategy. Their fee ranges from $40 to $75 an hour.

At the top are specialists, copywriters who work exclusively within a certain industry or on a special type of copy. Some of the highest paid copywriting specialties include financial, medical, industrial, high-tech, annual reports, and direct mail. Top copywriters charge anywhere from $75 to $150 an hour.

What will copywriting cost by the project? For a small booklet or folded brochure designed to fit in a standard business envelope, expect to pay anywhere from $500 to $1,500. For a full-size brochure (8½″ × 11″ pages), the cost ranges from $300 to $700 per page.

For a catalog, expect to pay anywhere from $25 to $200 per item, or $400 to $600 per page. Annual reports are the most ambitious projects and can run from $7,000 to $10 ,000.

Graphic artists

Graphic artists perform three basic services: design, mechanicals, and illustration. Some do all three; others, just one or two. That's something you want to find out before you hire them.

Design involves determining the appearance of the printed page: where the photos, type, and headlines are positioned; the size and style of the typography; the cropping and size of photos and illustrations; the number of columns of text and the size of the page; and the use of color.

The final product of design is a sketch of what the pages of the finished printed piece will look like. This sketch is known as a *comprehensive* or *comp*. For design services, artists charge anywhere from $40 to $125 an hour.

The next step is to render the comprehensive in a format that is *camera-ready*, meaning it can be taken to a printer and reproduced on a printing press. The traditional format for camera-ready art used to be a *mechanical*, a paste-up of typeset body copy, headlines, and visuals, ready to be reproduced on a printing press. The type was literally cut apart with a knife and pasted to a piece of stiff cardboard.

Now, with computers using page layout software such as Quark or PageMaker, many artists do the layout on a computer screen and produce camera-ready output directly from their PCs.

Many printers accept computer disks that they convert to film for printing on a press. Or the graphic designer can take the disk to a service bureau, which will use a high-resolution image-setter to produce film or high-resolution printouts for the printer. Whereas pasting up the mechanicals used to be considered a lower-skill task than planning layouts, today most artists using computers not only design layouts, but also give you camera-ready output in one or more formats.

If your brochure has drawings, you'll also need an illustrator. Hourly fees vary widely, from $50 to $100 or more, depending on the type of illustration required. Someone who produces elaborate full-color oil paintings is likely to get a higher fee than an artist who draws simple black-and-white line sketches.

Most illustrations are commissioned by the project, however, and not by the hour. Again, price is a complex function and depends on your ability to define precisely what it is you want the artist to produce. A simple line graph can be bought for $75 to $125. A nice color schematic or airbrush sketch of a piece of industrial equipment can run $400 to $800. A color portrait of your company's board of directors can cost $1,000.

When selecting an illustrator or designer, take a look at her or his portfolio (sample case of work). Pick someone whose style matches what you had in mind for your own brochure.

Photographers

Many business people feel that photography does not require much skill and that anyone can take good pictures. They are wrong. Photographers are highly skilled professionals. Many of the photos we take ourselves may look passable when viewed as a print. But when printed in a brochure, their flaws become evident, and you then see why you should have used a professional photographer in the first place.

Photographers charge by the hour, by the day, or by the project. Day rates range from $400 to $2,000 or more; $500 to $1,000 is typical.

When a photographer quotes you a fee, ask whether it includes film, processing, props, and other materials. These incidentals can add up to a hefty amount on the final bill, so if they're not included try to get a rough estimate of what they'll cost.

Another issue is ownership rights. Photographer fees have traditionally entitled buyers to limited usage of the photo in a specific brochure or promotion, with the rights (ownership) of the photo retained by the photographer.

In today's competitive and cost-conscious marketplace, many clients now insist that, for the fee they pay, they get unlimited use of the photos and the photographer gives up all rights; the photo becomes the client's exclusive property.

Be sure to discuss the issue of usage and ownership up front, and keep in mind that everything is negotiable. I think it is important for clients to have unlimited usage of all photos they pay to have taken, and I urge you to insist on this.

If you need one or two shots at a single location, the job can probably be done in a day. If you can arrange to have all your photos shot in a single location, thus eliminating the need for the photographer to do much traveling, you'll save a lot of money.

As with artists and writers, choose a photographer whose specialty, style, and level of experience meet your needs and your budget. A photographer specializing in food or fashion may charge as much as $2,500 for a single color photo. But an industrial photographer can take a competent photo of your submersible pump and charge you only $250 for it.

Whatever your needs, be sure to pick a photographer with experience shooting for advertising and promotion. Wedding photographers and those who take family portraits for a living aren't the ones you want for your brochure.

Desktop Publishing Services

In recent years, with the explosive growth in desktop publishing, a new category of vendor has been created, the desktop publishing company.

These companies do work similar to graphic design studios or free-lance graphic artists, designing layouts and producing camera-ready mechanicals for brochures and other promo pieces. Their distinguishing characteristic is that all work is done on desktop microcomputers, using page layout, illustration, fonts, laser printers, optical scanners, modems, and other desktop publishing hardware and software.

Interestingly, since most traditional design studios and graphic artists are moving from manual art to desktop computer systems, the services they offer are pretty similar to those of desktop publishers. Then what's the difference?

Desktop publishing companies are usually, but not always, free-lancers—individuals with a Macintosh or other computer and appropriate software. Desktop publishers are often more computer-oriented than art-oriented, so their work is often more straightforward, and less innovative or creative.

They also tend to work on simpler projects, such as black-and-white fliers, small brochures, and so on, whereas design firms handle full-color brochures, annual reports, and larger, more complex projects.

Most desktop publishing firms work on an hourly rate ranging from $25 to $65 an hour. Project estimates are given based on the number of hours estimated to complete the job. Desktop publishers are usually 20 to 40 percent less costly than companies calling themselves "design studios" or "graphic arts studios."

Service Bureaus

Service bureaus are firms that own expensive equipment used to convert computer output to high-resolution film or mechanicals to be reproduced on a printing press.

The main type of machine is an *image setter*, which produces either hard-copy printouts or film at resolutions many times higher than the 300 to 600 dots per inch that can be achieved using an ordinary laser printer.

You will often hear graphics people refer to this equipment as "Linotronics." Linotronics is the brand name of a specific image setter.

Many service bureaus can convert computer diskettes to formats acceptable to their image setters, saving you the task of formatting or converting your disk. Some have optical scanners that can scan typewritten output and convert it to computer-readable form.

Design studios or other vendors you hire to do graphics will handle taking their work to the service bureau for you, in most cases. If you are producing your own material, ask colleagues or artists for the name of a reliable service bureau near you.

Typographers

Typographers use special machines to produce type. Type is black lettering printed on photographic paper; the lettering can be pasted up on a stiff cardboard and reproduced on a printing press for use in books, catalogs, magazines, newspapers, advertisements, brochures, and other printed matter.

With the advent of desktop publishing, especially high-resolution laser printers and the growing number of fonts (type styles) available on desktop systems, traditional phototypesetting is rapidly becoming a thing of the past. Most typesetting companies have become service bureaus; only a few still set type from typewritten manuscripts. Not many graphic artists today still cut type apart and paste it on boards by hand; most do their page layouts using software and a PC.

Printers

If you have a typewritten or desktop-published technical manual or a one-page black-and-white flier, you may be able to get away with copying it on the office photocopier. But any piece of literature used to promote your organization or your product should be reproduced by a professional printer.

Selecting a printer is a two-step process. The first step takes place at the beginning of the brochure production cycle, the second when the mechanical is finished and the brochure ready for printing.

In the first step, you call up half a dozen printers in your area. Explain the type of project you have in mind. The printers interested in handling the job will either stop by your office to show you samples of their work or have you come by their place to show you their operation first-hand.

Ask the printers to give you a rough estimate of what your proposed brochure will cost to print. They can't give you a firm quotation because price depends on a number of factors that haven't been decided yet, such as use of visuals, use of colors, and selection of paper stock. But they should be able to give a rough estimate based on your preliminary plans.

In the second stage, choose three printers whose work you liked and whose rough estimates were reasonable. Go to these printers with the finished mechanical and complete specifications for paper stock, colors, and number of copies to be printed. Ask them to give you a firm price for the job.

You'll usually pick the lowest estimate, but not always. If the price difference is small, other factors—quality of work, speed of delivery, even the personality of the printer—my make you decide in favor of someone who is slightly more expensive.

What will printing cost? It depends on the quantity and quality desired and on the complexity of the job. You can print 500 one-page fliers for $60. The printing bill on a fancy annual report or color brochure can run thousands of dollars. The way you know that you're paying a fair price for printing is to get *three* estimates on every job from reliable sources you can trust.

How to Select Outside Vendors

How do you pick the right writer, photographer, artist, desktop publisher, printer? Here are some tips to help you make the proper selection.

■ **Ask around**

The easiest way to find the service you need is to go to a colleague and say, "I'm putting together a brochure and I need a good designer and photographer. Is there anyone you can recommend?"

Organizations in your community that produce printed literature already know who the best writers, artists, photographers, printers, and typesetters are. When you find a supplier through referral, you have the advantage of knowing that the supplier has at least one satisfied customer.

If no one can recommend a good supplier to you, you can go to outside sources: the Yellow Pages, trade magazines, and the industry directories listed at the end of this chapter.

■ **Look for quality**

Your literature doesn't have to be complex, expensive, or elegant. But it should be crisp, sharp, and professional. Shoddy work, whether in graphics, writing, photography, or printing, can ruin an otherwise fine piece.

When you're evaluating an outside supplier, check the work. If he's a writer, read his sample brochures and catalogs. If she's a photographer, carefully examine her photo portfolio. You'll be amazed at how quality varies from supplier to supplier.

■ **Find someone with experience in your business**

Advertising professionals specialize in different areas and industries: fundraising, political, direct mail, industrial, fashion, retail, publishing, financial.

All else being equal, it makes sense to pick a vendor with experience in your area. The vendor's prior knowledge of your industry means you have to spend less time educating her. Also, her experiences with other companies similar to yours increase her value as an advisor and consultant to you.

■ **Look for a style that fits your corporate identity**

Your organization, no matter how small, has an identity and a style all its own. If yours is a big organization, this corporate identity is shaped by the structure and direction of the company as a whole. If it's a smaller, entrepreneurial firm, the style may well be dictated entirely by the personality of the owner.

Short of a complete overhaul of your corporate identity (and there are high-priced firms and consultants that specialize in giving such overhauls), you usually want your printed literature to enhance your image, not distort it. That's why you should choose advertising professionals whose style in graphics and writing meshes with your own.

If you like dignified, tasteful sales literature, pick a designer whose portfolio is full of dignified, tasteful sales literature. If you want your literature to communicate an image of corporate bigness, choose the designer who specializes in creating annual reports and capabilities brochures for Fortune 500 corporations.

But please note that a strange thing happens to smaller businesses when they get a little extra money in the advertising budget: They see fancy full-color brochures, gold-embossed mailers, and fat annual reports produced by big corporations. And they say, "This stuff sure looks great—why don't we do some brochures like this?"

That's a mistake. The look, tone, and image of your promotional literature should be dictated by your product and your market, not by what other companies in other businesses are doing.

Producing literature that's too fancy for its purpose and audience is a waste of money. And it can even hurt sales: Your customers look at your overdone literature and wonder whether you really understand your market and its needs.

■ **Don't overbook outside talent**

Hire free-lancers, vendors, and consultants whose credentials, talents, and fees fit the job and the budget.

Top advertising photographers, for example, get $1,200 or more a day. This may be worth the fee for a corporate ad running in *Forbes* or *Business Week*. But it's overkill for putting a picture of the company picnic in the employee newsletter. A gifted amateur or a competent publicity photographer could take a few informal shots of the company baseball team for one-fifth of what the advertising photographer would charge.

■ **Examine the supplier's client list**

Ask to see a list of clients the supplier has worked for recently. A good supplier has an active list of many clients. If a professional is unable to give you a list of clients, it may mean he or she is just starting out and may be too inexperienced to handle your assignment.

To make sure you're hiring a reliable supplier, you can call a couple of the companies on the client list. If the list doesn't include the names and phone numbers of the people the supplier worked with, ask the supplier to give you a couple of references to call. When you call, ask the references if they were satisfied with the supplier's work. Did the supplier do a top-quality job? Was he or she easy to work with, or a prima donna? Were deadlines met? Did the final bill match the original estimate? And, the most important question: Would you hire this supplier again? If the answer is no, or if it's yes but with some hesitation, you might want to check out a few more suppliers before you make your choice.

■ **Provide complete information**

The two most common questions advertisers ask advertising professionals are "Can you do it?" and "What will it cost?" (The third most common is "How long will it take?") The more information you can give the professional, the more accurate the estimate you'll receive.

Estimating the cost and amount of work involved in writing or designing a brochure is a difficult thing. When you call on, say, a plumber, the plumber can take a look at your leaky toilet and see precisely how much work is involved. But the brochure producer can't know exactly what is involved, because you don't yet know exactly how you want the finished piece to look and read.

You can help suppliers estimate the job by being as specific and complete as possible. For example, the printer doesn't expect you to name the brand of paper stock you want to use, but you could bring along samples of brochures you've collected to give an idea of the approximate weight, finish, and appearance of the paper you want for your brochure.

At the end of Chapter 2, I gave you a literature specification sheet to help you plan your sales literature. Fill in this sheet as completely as possible, make copies, and distribute it to vendors whom you're thinking of hiring. The sheet will give them most of the information they'll need to quote a price on the job; and what they don't know, they'll ask.

■ **Talk about price up front**

It's wise to discuss money with your vendors *before* you hire them. Find out the supplier's fee and get a written estimate. If the fee is firm, the agreement between the two of you should say so.

Your agreement or purchase order should also spell out the terms and conditions of the deal: when the money is to be paid, whether there are additional charges for changes, what happens if you aren't satisfied with the work.

If the estimate is just that, an estimate, find out how much it can vary. If the supplier is working by the day or by the hour, ask for an estimate of how many days or hours it will take to complete the job.

When you come to terms, put it in writing. You can send a purchase order or a letter of authorization to the supplier, or you can ask the supplier to send you a letter or contract that you both sign. A written agreement clearly spells out what is expected from both you and the vendor and helps avoid misunderstandings, which can lead to arguments, ill will, collection agencies, or even court.

How to Get the Best Results from Vendors

Here are some tips for getting the best work out of your free-lancers, agencies, and other outside resources.

■ **Provide thorough guidelines and instructions**

The more precisely you communicate what you're looking for, the closer the finished brochure will be to the vision you had in mind when you started out.

The biggest problem in advertising is that clients don't tell their suppliers what they expect from them, and the suppliers don't ask the questions they should ask to find out what the client wants. The result is dissatisfied clients, aggravation, and time and money lost in redoing work that doesn't meet the advertiser's specifications.

As the client, you can avoid this by giving specific and complete briefings to all your suppliers. The artist, for example, needs to know any preferences you have concerning the design: page size, number of pages, type of paper stock, use of color, use of photos and illustrations, method of folding or binding, and overall graphic look and style. You may hate brown, but the artist won't know to stay away from brown unless you make that clear. That's why it helps to sit down with the artist and explain what you have in mind before he or she starts designing the piece. Another helpful technique is to bring along sample brochures to illustrate a particular typeface, design technique, page layout, or other graphic element that has caught your fancy.

The writer also requires a thorough briefing. Ideally, you should collect all previously published material on the product and give it to your writer as background information. This material can include ads, brochures, catalogs, annual reports, press releases, article clippings, product manuals, marketing plans, package labels, diagrams, manufacturer's specification sheets, charts, presentations, speeches, and slide-show and film scripts. Once the writer studies this material, 80 percent of the information needed to write your piece will be in hand. And the other 20 percent can be obtained by asking a few well-directed questions.

Printers, ad agency account executives, consultants, and illustrators will also appreciate a thorough briefing on the project. The more they know, the better the job they'll do.

■ Be available

Although your suppliers will probably work without direct supervision, they'll need to confer with you from time to time. Be available when they want to discuss an idea, show you a layout, or ask questions about the project. And if they submit work for you to review, approve it or hand it back for revision as soon as you can. There are many stages during a project where the outside vendor can't proceed without your input or authorization. If you're not available to review material or provide guidance, the project will be delayed until your suppliers hear from you.

One person from your company, either you or your representative, should be the coordinator for the project and act as liaison between your organization and any outside suppliers. To ensure speedy completion of the job, the coordinator should make it her or his business to be available to outside vendors at all times.

■ Don't meddle

There's a difference between being available and being a meddler, and it's the difference between being a good client and being a bad one. The good client helps the agency or free-lancers when they need it and provides guidance when they ask for it. The bad client, the meddler, tells the agency or free-lancers how to do their job or, worse, tries to do it for them. Martin Gross, creative director of Doremus Direct, wrote about this in an article in *DM News* (Nov. 15, 1983):

> If you meddle with the judgments and the execution of the freelancer, you're not getting what you've paid for. Rewriting, redesigning, and second-guessing are wasteful practices. If you're unhappy with the job, speak up early.

If you don't like the copy, don't rewrite it. Instead, tell the writer what's wrong with the copy and have her fix it. And don't go out and buy a sketch pad because you think the artist's layout is organized the wrong way. Instead, tell the artist how you want it organized and let him redo the layout.

■ Be open to new ideas

As the person paying the bills, you're entitled to have it your own way. The final decisions on copy, art, design, layout, and printing are yours.

However, keep in mind that you've hired a team of experts, experts whose only business is the production of advertising materials. If they suggest new ideas, or want to handle the project somewhat differently than what you had in mind, don't instantly reject these new ideas. Instead, listen carefully and think about the suggestions. Maybe they'll work better than your version. Maybe not. But you're paying these people for their ideas; why not get your money's worth? Their advice is based on years of experience in an area that's pretty much "Greek" to you; often, the agency or free-lancer has encountered your type of problem before and already knows how to solve it.

■ **Make your criticism constructive**

I've never been involved in a brochure project where the client didn't want some changes made somewhere along the way. Sometimes the changes are minor and inconsequential. Sometimes they amount to a major overhaul and drastically change the nature of the finished piece. More often, the revisions lie somewhere between these two extremes.

When you want changes made, be as specific as possible. If you say, "I don't like it" or "it doesn't send me" or something equally vague, the writer and artist have nothing to go on. They know only that you're displeased. What they don't know is how to make it right.

If the copy needs revision, go through the manuscript with a red pencil and write in corrections and suggestions. This doesn't mean rewriting copy; it does mean you should supply missing facts and correct wrong ones.

Be specific with changes. If the writer has described the function of your product incorrectly, it means he or she doesn't understand how the product works. So if you just write in the margin, "system operation section WRONG!!!" the writer will have no way of knowing how to correct the error. You can solve this by attaching a brief description of the operation to the manuscript or by telling the writer where to find the missing facts ("see page 3 of old brochure for correct explanation of operations").

Writers and artists are people, too. And creative types often have more fragile egos than the general population. So it pays to be tactful when you ask an artist or writer for revisions. Instead of being brusk and negative in your criticisms, be warm, supportive, and positive.

Don't say to your artist, "I can't accept a layout like this! The type is too small, there's too much text on the pages, and the whole thing looks cluttered. Don't you know how to use white space?" Instead, say, "First, let me thank you for getting this done so quickly. Basically, it looks good, and there are only a few changes we need to make. Let's take a look...."

As a manager, you know that your employees perform well when they're treated decently. Apply the same principle to outside agencies and free-lancers, and you'll get their best effort on your brochure.

■ **Don't change your mind in midstream**

The time to agonize over the style and type of literature you want is before your hired help goes to work on it, not after. If you change your mind in midstream, you'll have to pay the price of redoing the work. Your indecisiveness will also frustrate the people working on your account and cause them to put less than their best effort forward on your behalf.

If you have to make changes, make them early in the production cycle. As the brochure nears completion, even minor changes become extremely costly. For example, if you change the text while it's in manuscript form, the only cost is the writer's revision time. But changing text once the type is set means setting new type and possibly redoing page layouts. Most design studios or graphic designers will charge you their hourly rate, above and beyond the agreed-upon fee, for "AAs" or "author's alterations" (changes made in the layout after copy and design have already been approved).

To avoid these extra charges, make sure everyone in your organization has approved the work submitted by your vendors before you authorize the vendors to go on to the next step. Once you approve something, stick with that decision and don't change your mind unless it's absolutely necessary.

■ **Simplify the review process**

Most organizations put their promotional literature through an approval cycle before it can be published. The fewer people involved in the review process, the better. If the brochure is rewritten and redesigned by a corporate committee, it will lose its vitality, originality, and selling power; the result will be a bland piece of paper that pleases your management but fails to stir the buying public. As the saying goes, "A moose is a cow designed by committee."

I've seen situations where 15 people were required to sign off on a document before it could be published. For the best results, you should limit the number of reviewers to three: a person who knows the product from a technical point of view (an engineer, scientist, or researcher), the person responsible for the marketing of the product (a product manager, marketing manager, brand manager, or sales manager), and the person in charge of the company's literature program (an advertising manager, communications manager, or perhaps the division or company president). Any more than that is just excess baggage.

■ **Don't nitpick**

If you have the task of reviewing a brochure manuscript and layout, concentrate your criticisms on the important issues: technical accuracy, completeness of content, organization, persuasiveness, readability, format, use of visuals, and overall appearance. Don't fuss with little things that are largely a matter of subjective judgment: whether the writer should have used a comma instead of a semicolon, or whether the chairman of the board should appear in a striped or a polka-dot tie. When you make changes, make changes of substance. Don't nitpick the copy and layout to death.

■ Don't waste time

Avoid unnecessary meetings, paperwork, correspondence, and conferences. Limit contact with outside vendors to necessary communication. These folks are in business to make a profit, and the more of their time you waste, the less profitable your business will be to them. And if your business is not profitable, they will not devote their best efforts to it.

Some clients have the bad habit of calling up their agency or free-lancer half a dozen times a day to ask, "How's it going?" Others expect the agency account executive or free-lancer to come in for a conference every time they want to change a word of copy or replace a photo. You should do neither. Leave your vendors alone, let them do their job, don't pester, and they'll be grateful for it. That gratitude will translate into more time spent on your account.

■ Pay your bills on time

Few things make ad agencies and free-lancers as unhappy as not being paid on time. Unpaid invoices put a strain on the supplier/client relationship, and this strain can affect the quality of the work. So pay your bills on time; your vendors will love you for it.

How to Find Vendors

Here are some sources to help you locate the suppliers you need:

- *Standard Directory of Advertising Agencies: The Agency Red Book*, published by the National Register Publishing Company, Inc., 5201 Old Orchard Road, Skokie, IL 60077, (312) 256-6067. This directory lists 4,400 advertising agencies. For each agency, the *Red Book* reports agency income, number of employees, key accounts, personnel, and the addresses and phone numbers of its offices. The Red Book is available in most libraries.

- *O'Dwyer's Directory of Public Relations Firms*, 271 Madison Avenue, New York, NY 10016, (212) 679-2471. Lists 1,200 public relations firms. Available in most libraries.

- *The Creative Black Book*, published by Friendly Publications, Inc., 401 Park Avenue South, New York, NY 10016, (212) 684-4255. Lists thousands of photographers, illustrators, graphic designers, TV producers, ad agencies, typographers, audio-visual suppliers, retouchers, and printers. Available by mail order through the publisher. Can also be found in major bookstores.

- *Adweek/Art Directors' Index*, copublished by RotoVision S.A. and Adweek, 820 Second Avenue, New York, NY 10017, (212) 661-8080. Lists illustrators, graphic designers, photographers, stock photography houses, artist's representatives, TV producers and directors, printers, art directors, audio-visual services, typographers, and copywriters. Available from the publisher.

- *Adweek*, 820 Second Avenue, New York, NY 10017, (212) 661-8080. Weekly advertising magazine. Has a special advertising section for creative services (including free-lance copywriting and graphic design). Available by subscription and at some newsstands.

- Also check your local Yellow Pages for listings under Advertising Agencies, Public Relations Firms, Graphic Design Studios, Artists, Illustrators, Writers, Copywriters, Photographers, Phototypesetters, Typographers, and Printers.

CHAPTER FOUR

TELLING YOUR STORY: THE OUTLINE

An outline is an informal description of the contents of a planned piece of writing, whether a brochure, catalog, booklet, article, book, manual, or any other document you want to produce.

I know the word outline gives you a twinge of anxiety. It dredges up memories of dusty schoolrooms where teachers had you make endless outlines as academic exercises. But to the brochure writer, an outline is no academic exercise; it's a tool that helps the writer—and the client—plan and produce a brochure that says what the advertiser wants it to say.

Outlines as taught in elementary schools were rigid, useless lists of facts locked into a system of Roman and Arabic numerals and upper- and lowercase letters. Remember, for example, how you couldn't have a IIA unless you had a IIB? Such restrictions make people shy away from academic outlines—and rightly so.

But a brochure outline need not follow any particular format. It can be as formal or informal, as simple or complex, as you like. A numbered list, a series of bulleted items, doodles, rough notes, a stack of index cards—use whatever format suits you. The outline helps you divide the writing project into many smaller, easy-to-handle pieces and parts.

The level of detail included in the outline depends on what you're comfortable with. Some people like to work from a short list of the general topics to be included in the brochure. Others make a point-by-point outline covering every single fact. An intermediate step is a rough outline with some notes jotted down describing in brief the contents of each section.

The one danger is getting locked into an outline that doesn't work. That's why an outline should be treated as a tool, not as a commandment etched in stone. For example, your outline may include a product specification under one section, but during the writing you discover that this specification would fit better in a different section. Go ahead and make the change! Use the outline as a guide, but don't get trapped in it.

That's how I tackled the task of writing this book. I started with a list of the chapters in the order they would appear. But, because of the book's length, I felt I needed a more detailed guideline, and so under each chapter I added a list of sections and their headings. When I began to write, I discovered that some new sections needed to be added, while other sections could be combined or cut altogether. I made these changes, and so the finished book doesn't follow my original outline to the letter. But it's pretty close to the outline and without the outline, the book would have been much more difficult to organize and to write.

The best way of approaching the project is for you, the advertiser, to come up with some idea of what you'd like to put in your brochure. After all, you've lived with the product or service or idea for a long time. No one knows better than you what needs to be said about it. Your outline doesn't have to be long or formal or typed in any "proper" outline format. Just make a short list of the topics you think should be covered by the literature. Figure 4.1 is a checklist of some of the possible topics you might want to include in your outline.

If the assignment is to update or redo an existing brochure, you can create a working outline simply by going through a copy of the brochure and noting any changes directly on the page. Cross out blocks of copy that will be dropped from the new version. Use a yellow marker to highlight copy you particularly like and want to reuse in the new brochure. Make notes in pen or pencil in the margins to indicate the extent and nature of desired changes. Then give this marked-up copy to your writer for reference during your first meeting.

The writer is given the rough outline along with the other background material on the project (previous ads, brochures, catalog descriptions, specification sheets, and other published material as discussed in Chapter 3). The writer's task is to come back with a more detailed and complete outline that reflects the content you are looking for in your new brochure.

Review the writer's outline. Add topics that are missing. Delete topics that aren't necessary. Suggest a different order for the material if that makes sense. Then, when everybody is comfortable with the outline, the writer can proceed to write a first draft of the brochure text.

The rest of this chapter contains generic or model outlines for some of the most common types of sales literature: product brochures, service brochures, corporate capabilities brochures, case histories, annual reports, and several others. These outlines can serve as a guide to shaping the content of your own promotional literature.

Of course, don't feel obligated to follow these model outlines. If you find a better way of organizing your material, use it! Each project is different, and you shouldn't force your own ideas into an overly simplistic formula. The sample outlines should be used as rough guidelines only.

Figure 4.1   A checklist of items to include in your product literature.

_____ Accessories	_____ Delivery terms
_____ Accuracy	_____ Design
_____ Address	_____ Dimensions
_____ Appearance	_____ Directions to store
_____ Applications	_____ Discounts
_____ Assembly required	_____ Documentation
_____ Availability	_____ Ease of use
_____ Batteries required	_____ Effectiveness
_____ Biographies of key personnel	_____ Efficiency rating
_____ Built-in diagnostics (self-test)	_____ Energy consumption
_____ Byproducts	_____ Enhancements and improve-
_____ Capabilities	ments
_____ Capacity	_____ Fax numbers
_____ Certifications, seals of	_____ Field service
approval	_____ Field test results
_____ Colors	_____ Finishes
_____ Comparison with other	_____ Functions
products	_____ Guarantee
_____ Components	_____ History
_____ Configurations	_____ How it works
_____ Construction	_____ Installation instructions
_____ Controls and instrumentation	_____ International offices
_____ Cost savings	_____ Laboratory performance
_____ Corrosion resistance	_____ Limitations
_____ Credit cards accepted	_____ Location
_____ Customer list	_____ Maintenance
_____ Customer testimonials	_____ Manufacturing capabilities
_____ Customization available	_____ Materials of construction
_____ Dealer network	_____ Method of manufacture
_____ Delivery (how long does it	_____ Method of operation
take?)	_____ Models available

Figure 4.1   Continued.

_____ Model numbers
_____ MTBF ("mean time between failures" reliability rating)
_____ MTTR ("mean time to repair"; how quickly repairs can be made)
_____ Name of organization
_____ Name of product
_____ Name of service
_____ No moving parts
_____ Number of units sold
_____ Number of years in business
_____ Operating costs
_____ Operating range
_____ Options
_____ Ordering information
_____ Parent company
_____ Parts
_____ Performance
_____ Pilot plant
_____ Pollution controls
_____ Portability
_____ Power requirements
_____ Price
_____ Problems solved by product
_____ Product life
_____ Product line
_____ Purchase price
_____ Quality control
_____ Refund policy
_____ Reliability
_____ Repair tips
_____ Replacement parts
_____ Refills

_____ Retrofits
_____ Safety features
_____ Selection guide
_____ Service
_____ Shape
_____ Shipping and handling
_____ Sizes
_____ Space required
_____ Specifications
_____ Speed
_____ State of the art (is it new?)
_____ Storage
_____ Strength
_____ Styles
_____ Target market (type of customer product is designed for)
_____ Technical support
_____ Telephone number
_____ Telex number
_____ Temperature range
_____ Terms
_____ Time savings
_____ Training
_____ Uses
_____ Warehouse locations
_____ Warranty
_____ Weight
_____ Years in business
_____ Others: _____
_____
_____
_____
_____

Product Brochures

The most common type of promotional literature is the brochure describing a product.

Years ago, product brochures were used mainly by industrial manufacturers for answering inquiries. But today's consumer has a great hunger for product information, and so many more brochures are being written about *consumer* products: telephones, room heaters, venetian blinds, microwave ovens, VCRs, personal computers, software, automobiles, home improvement products, exercise equipment, CD players, pianos, even perfume and health care products.

The size of the brochure depends upon the level of detail. For simpler products, you can use a small pamphlet or "slim-jim" brochure. This is made by taking an 8½″ × 11″ (letter size) or 8½″ × 14″ (legal size) sheet (or smaller) and folding it two or three times into four, six, or eight panels (see Figure 4.2).

Figure 4.2   A single sheet of paper can be folded in a variety of ways to make a four-, six-, or eight-panel brochure.

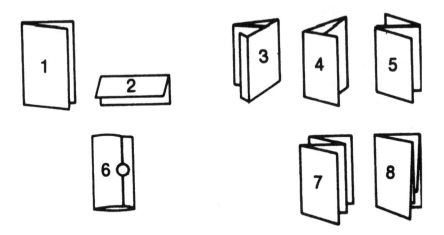

For complex products and lengthier sales pitches, product brochures use full-size pages and usually range from 2 to 8 pages, with 4 being the average. And some very technical brochures can be 12, 16, or even 20 or more pages.

The content varies with the product, the audience, and the sales goal of the piece. Below is a fairly comprehensive outline, the kind you might use for a larger product brochure. If you're doing a smaller piece, you could delete some of these topics or treat them in brief.

- *Introduction*—A capsule description of what the product is and why the reader should be interested in it.

- *Benefits*—A list of reasons why the customer should buy the product.

- *Features*—Highlights of important product features that set the product apart from the competition.

- *"How it works"*—A description of how the product works and what it can do. This section can include the results of any tests that demonstrate the product's superiority.

- *Types of users (markets)*—This section describes the special markets the product is designed for. A wastewater plant, for example, might be sold to municipalities, utilities, and industrial manufacturers—three separate and distinct markets, each with its own special set of requirements.

This section can also include a list of the names of well-known people or organizations that use and endorse your product.

- *Applications*—Descriptions of the various applications in which the product can be used.

- *Product availability*—Lists models, sizes, materials of construction, colors, finishes, options, accessories, and all the variations in which the product can be ordered. This section can also include charts, graphs, formulas, tables, or other guidelines to aid the reader in product selection.

- *Pricing*—Information on what the product costs, including prices for accessories, various models and sizes, quantity discounts, and shipping and handling.

- *Technical specifications*—Electrical requirements, power consumption, resistance to moisture, temperature range, operating conditions, cleaning methods, storage conditions, chemical properties, product life, and other characteristics and limitations of the product.

- *Questions and answers*—Answers to frequently asked questions about the product. Includes information not found in other sections.

- *Company description*—A brief biography of the manufacturer, written to show the reader that the product is backed by a solid, reputable organization that won't go out of business.

- *Product support*—Information on delivery, installation, training, maintenance, service, and guarantees.

- *"The next step"*—Instructions on how to order the product (or on how to get more information on the product).

Use this outline as a guide, but don't feel obligated to include all the sections or stick with this order. A brochure on an automobile, for example, probably shouldn't include the price, because car salesmen love to make deals and don't want to be locked into a fixed price.

Service Brochures

In many ways, writing a service brochure is harder than writing a product brochure.

The reason is that the product brochure describes an existing object with tangible features and benefits. To write the brochure, you simply describe the product and what it can do.

But selling a service involves selling intangibles: the reputation of the service organization, the expertise of its people, the benefits of using the service, the quality of the service versus competing services. You have to get the reader to trust you, because you can't point to a package and say, "There's what we're selling." You have to write copy on a somewhat more personal level, because you're really selling people and their talents.

- *Introduction*—Outlines the services offered, types of clients handled, and the reasons why the reader should be interested in the service.

- *Services offered*—Detailed descriptions of the various services offered by the firm.

- *Benefits*—Descriptions of what readers will gain from the service and why they should engage your firm instead of the competition.

- *Background information*—Background information on the problems the service is designed to solve. This section can offer free advice on how to evaluate the problem and how to select professional help. Such free information, while not a direct sales pitch, adds to the value of the brochure and causes readers to hold on to your literature.

- *Methodology*—Outlines the service firm's method of doing business with clients.

- *Client list*—A list of well-known people or organizations who have used the firm's services.

- *Testimonials*—statements of endorsement from selected clients. Testimonials are usually written in the client's own words and attributed to a specific person or organization.

- *Fees and terms*—Describes the fees for each service and the terms and method of payment required. Also includes whatever guarantee the service firm offers its clients.

- *Biographical information*—Capsule biographies highlighting the credentials of the key employees plus an overall capsule biography of the firm.

- *"The next step"*—Instructions on what to do next if you are interested in hiring the firm or learning more about their services.

Corporate Capabilities Brochures

Opinions are mixed on whether corporate brochures are useful. Some people claim that corporate brochures are an exercise in self-flattery, and that no one reads them except those in the company that publishes it. Others see the corporate brochure as a useful tool for quickly communicating the message of who you are to customers, prospects, distributors, new employees, vendors, the press, and the financial community.

In no other piece of literature (except annual reports) do you have to be as image-conscious as in the corporate brochure—simply because it is the statement that says who you are, what you do, and what you're like. An image-conscious brochure doesn't necessarily have to be lavish or expensive.

But the look of the design and tone of the copy should mirror and enhance the image you want to project.

- The business (or businesses) the company is engaged in
- The corporate structure (parent company, other members of the family, subsidiaries)
- Addresses and phone numbers of all offices, branches, and representatives
- Names and titles of major corporate officers
- History
- Plants and other facilities
- Geographical coverage
- Major markets
- Distribution systems
- Sales
- Ranking in its field relative to competition
- Extent of stock distribution
- Earnings record
- Dividends record
- Number of employees
- Employee benefits
- Noteworthy employees (e.g., scientists, inventors)
- Inventions
- Significant achievements
- Research and development
- Quality control practices
- Compliance with important standards, guidelines, and regulations (e.g., compliance with ISO 9000 quality standards, participation in Responsible Care environmental safety programs, etc.)
- Actions with respect to the environment
- Contributions (to art, public welfare, etc.)
- Awards
- Policies
- Plans

Catalogs

The catalog is a comprehensive piece of literature describing all of the products a company sells. "Resting on the table in farm, suburban or city home, the...catalog functions like a one-stop shopping center," writes Julien Elfenbein in his book *Business Letters and Communications*.

A catalog contains numerous product descriptions. The two key issues in organizing a catalog are (1) the information to include in each product description and (2) the order in which to organize product descriptions.

In addition to product listings, a catalog my also have a letter from the manufacturer, an introduction, a table of contents, an index, a page describing conditions and terms, and, if it's a mail-order catalog, a form and reply envelope you can use to order products by mail.

In each product description you can include the following information:

- Name of the product
- Physical description
- Features and benefits
- Explanation of how it works
- Weight
- Dimensions, including choice of sizes available
- Price, including quantity discounts
- Quantities available
- Colors available
- Shape
- Styles
- Applications
- Tips on selection
- Tips on usage
- Packaging
- Shipping information
- Safety precautions
- Quality
- Materials of construction
- Efficiency
- Maintenance and repair methods
- Cost savings
- Service available
- Nearest distributors

The amount of information to be included depends on the space available. Most catalog listings are limited to a quarter page or less, and so you have to be extra concise, boiling copy down to a few essential sales points. Other catalog marketers find that by putting fewer items in their catalog, or by printing a bigger catalog, they can devote more copy to each product and increase sales as a result.

Organizing your catalog

The product descriptions can be ordered according to one of the eleven organization principles listed below. The choice of which to use depends on your product line, the size of the catalog, and your audience's buying habits.

■ By catalog hot spots
Mail-order catalog marketers can measure the sales generated by every page and every item in their catalogs. They've discovered that certain pages generate more sales than others.

According to the Performance Seminar Group, a company that gives seminars in advertising and marketing, these catalog "hot spots" are: the outside front cover, the outside back cover, the two-page spread inside the front cover, the two-page center spread, the two-page spread inside the back cover, the pages around the order form, and the pages around the ordering instructions. Other marketers have found that product descriptions printed directly on the order form also generate a higher rate of response than the average page. Based on this information, mail-order catalog marketers can generate more sales by putting their best-selling items on these hot pages.

■ By product demand
You can organize your catalog by the sales each product generates. Put your bestsellers up front and give each a full or half page. Slower-moving merchandise should appear at the back of the book and occupy a quarter page or less. Dead items are dropped altogether.

This organizational technique takes advantage of a principle first articulated by David Ogilvy: "Back your winners, and abandon your losers." It puts your promotional dollars where they'll do the most good. However, in large or highly technical product catalogs, it may create some confusion.

■ By applications
The Faultless Division of Axia Incorporated organized its caster catalog by application. The catalog has casters for general duty, light duty, light to

medium duty, heavy duty, textiles, scaffolds, floor trucks, and furniture.

Organizing according to application makes it easy for your customers to find the products that fit their needs. The disadvantage of this scheme is redundancy; many products handle multiple applications and must be listed or cross-referenced in more than one section of the catalog.

■ By function

A software catalog can be organized by the function each program performs: word processing, accounting, spread sheet, data base management, inventory, graphics, communications. This scheme obviously won't work in a catalog where all the products perform the same task (e.g., a catalog of pollution equipment, light switches, or safety valves).

■ By type of product

Radio Shack's consumer electronics catalogs are organized by product group: stereos on one page, car radios on the next, followed by VCRs, computers, tape recorders, and phone answering machines. This scheme is a natural for companies that carry multiple product lines.

■ By system hierarchy

This technique organizes products by the level at which each component fits into the overall system.

For example, if you manufacture computer hardware, your catalog can begin with the overall system you offer. Next come the major components: terminals, printers, plotters, disk drives, keyboards, processors. Then you get to the board level, showing various optional circuit boards you offer for memory expansion, interfaces, communications, instrument control, and other functions. Finally, you could even get down to the chip level, (if you sell chips as separate items). Supplies—paper, printer ribbons, diskettes, instruction manuals—could go in a separate section at the end of the catalog. This unit-subunit-subsubunit approach is ideal for manufacturers who sell both complete systems and their component parts.

■ By price

If you sell similar products that vary mainly in quality and price, you can organize your catalog by price categories. If your customers are concerned with savings, start with the cheapest items and work up. If you're selling to an upscale group willing to pay extra for top quality, start with the deluxe models and work your way down.

This technique is excellent for organizing a catalog of premiums and incentives. After all, a company searching for gifts and giveaways has a price range in mind, not necessarily a specific item.

■ By scarcity

If your catalog features hard-to-get items, consider putting them up front, even on the cover. This makes your catalog more valuable by offering buyers products they need but can't get elsewhere. Don't worry that these hard-to-find items aren't big sellers. When customers know your catalog has a stock of rare merchandise, and pull out your catalog to order it, they'll be more inclined to do their other buying from you, too.

■ By size

If you make one product and the basic selection criterion is size, it's only natural to organize your catalog according to dimensions, weight, horsepower, BTU's, diameter, or some other unit of measure. This is handy for catalogs selling boilers, motors, hoses, shipping drums, envelopes, light bulbs, air conditioners, and other equipment selected mainly on a size basis.

■ By model number

If you've worked out a sensible numbering system for your product line, organize your catalog by model number. If there's a simple meaning to your product coding, explain it at the start of the catalog. Don't rely solely on the numbers to describe your products; include headings and descriptive text as well.

■ Alphabetically

If no other organizational scheme works for you, you can always organize alphabetically. A tool catalog can start with adjustable strap clamps and angle plates and end with wing nuts and wrenches. A vitamin catalog can begin with Vitamin A and end with zinc.

Annual Reports

Annual reports are big documents. According to a survey conducted by the Graphic Arts Center, an Oregon printing firm, the average annual report is 44 pages long.

Most annual reports are divided into two major sections: descriptive and financial. The descriptive section reviews the company's activities for the year; the financial section provides the accounting information that the Securities and Exchange Commission requires publicly owned companies to disclose.

Here's an outline you can use for the descriptive portion of your annual report:

- *Financial highlights*—A table summarizing a few key financial figures (sales, net income, earnings per share of stock, cash dividends paid per share). If business was good, you can compare this year's figures to previous years to show a growth pattern.

- *Capsule corporate biography*—Three or four paragraphs that sum up the nature and mission of the corporation and touch on its key areas of business.

- *Table of contents*—Necessary to guide the reader through a lengthy document.

- *President's letter to shareholders*—Used to communicate key messages to shareholders, investors, and the business and financial communities. The President's Letter typically highlights company successes, acknowledges problems and tells how they are being solved, highlights earnings and stock performance, sums up the year's major triumphs, and talks about plans for the coming year.

- *Corporate overview*—A more detailed look at the structure, workings, and business functions of the corporation.

- *The year in review*—The bulk of the report's narrative and pictures reviews the year's business activities. Topics to be covered include products, markets, market share, revenues, expenses, sales, distribution, mergers, acquisitions, joint ventures, new areas of business, new tecnnology, new facilities, plant improvements, state of the industry, and strategic goals. This information is given for each of the corporation's divisions, subsidiaries, or operating units.

- *Photos*—Photos with captions provide visual interest and highlight people, products, projects, and other developments. Photos can be scattered throughout the report as well as placed in specific sections.

- *List of V.I.P.s*—Directors, corporate officers, and top management.

On the financial side, the Securities and Exchange Commission requires that annual reports satisfy certain guidelines, and your accounting firm can produce this information for you. Here's a list of what is typically included in the financial report:

- *Management discussion*—Your management's interpretation of the data in the financial report.

- *Accountant's report*—Signed statement made by your accountants verifying the accuracy of the financial report. There may also be notes on accounting methods used in preparing the report.

- *Statements of consolidated earnings*—Table showing the year's revenues, expenses, net earnings, and earnings per share.

- *Statements of consolidated retained earnings*—Beginning and year-end balances, net earnings, retained earnings, and cash dividends on common stock for the current year and for previous years.

- *Consolidated balance sheets*—Assets, liabilities, and stockholders' equities.

- *Statements of changes in consolidated financial position*—Source, use of, and increase or decrease in working capital.

- *Supplementary information on changing prices*—Explains the effect of inflation or recession on the firm's earnings and financial position.

- *Business segments*—Breakdown of revenue, earnings, assets, capital expenditures, and depreciation and amortization by corporate sub-unit.

- *Selected financial data*—A concise table summarizing key data (e.g., revenue, net earnings, dividends) for current and previous years.

- *Quarterly financial summaries*—Key financial data broken down by quarter for current and previous years.

- *Miscellaneous corporate information*—Date of shareholders' meetings, name of accounting firm, banks, stock exchange listing.

Case Histories

A case history is a product success story. It tells how a product or service was used to solve a problem, improve an operation, or save time and money. All case histories follow the same basic outline:

- *Problem*—What was the problem? How did it come about? Why? What were the unfortunate consequences of the problem?

- *Solution*—What solutions were considered and tried? What were the results? What solution finally worked? How was this solution arrived at? How was it implemented?

- *Results*—Was the problem cleared up? How are things now compared with the way they were before the solution was implemented? How have things improved since the product or service was used?

- *Conclusions and recommendations*—Why did the product or service work so well? Under what circumstances would it have worked better? Worse? What guidelines can be used to determine when the product or service should be applied to a similar problem in a different situation? What was learned about the performance and reliability of the product or service?

Newsletters

In his book *Mastering Graphics*, Jan White defines the newsletter as "a publication of limited circulation that is essentially informative in nature." "A true newsletter," he goes on to say, "is simple, informal, relaxed. Its effectiveness lies in the illusion it creates of being a person-to-person letter."

Newsletters deal with specialized subjects of interest to narrow groups of readers. A typical newsletter has anywhere from two to eight letter-size pages and is produced simply, usually typed on a typewriter, with a minimum of photos or illustrations. Fancier newsletters, often produced by large organizations, may be typeset and elaborately designed, but these are closer to being magazines than traditional newsletters.

There are two basic types of newsletters: subscription and promotional. Subscription newsletters are those people pay to receive. Publishing a successful newsletter can be a profitable venture, with annual subscription fees ranging from $65 to more than $600.

The other type of newsletter, the one we're discussing here, is the promotional newsletter. It is produced by an organization and distributed free of charge to customers, members, donors, sponsors, and prospects. The purpose of publishing the newsletter is to promote the organization's product, service, idea, or cause.

But the newsletter promotes in a subtle way: Instead of making a straight sales pitch, as would a product brochure or TV commercial, the newsletter's sell is somewhat softer. The readers receive a blend of useful information, ideas, and advice that is helpful in their lives or jobs. Some advertising messages may be woven into the newsletter, but only in moderation. Ideally, the newsletter should contain approximately 80 percent news and information and not more than 20 percent advertising or blatant promotion.

Rather than go for an order directly, the newsletter builds credibility with its audience over the long haul. Because the readers receive your promotional newsletter on a regular basis (as opposed to a one-shot promotion such as direct mail or a brochure), it builds recognition of your name and awareness of your products and services with that specific group of customers and prospects over time.

Stories in a newsletter can range in length from a few paragraphs up to a page, but most are shorter rather than longer. Unlike a brochure, in which each section builds on the previous one, each article in the newsletter is self-contained, so the order is not particularly important. Common sense dictates that you put the most important and interesting stories on page 1 and the less engaging copy on the inside pages.

What type of articles can you include in your newsletter? Anything goes—anything that is interesting to your reader and relevant to your organization's goals. Here's a partial list of some of the topics you can cover in your newsletter:

- Company news
- Industry news
- New products
- Product improvements
- New models
- New accessories
- New applications

- Tips on product selection
- Installation tips
- Maintenance and repair tips
- Troubleshooting guides
- Application notes (how to use the product)
- Explanatory articles (how the product works)
- Recent innovations in research and development
- Manufacturing success stories
- Quality control stories
- Case histories (product success stories)
- Technical information and tips
- Industry round-ups
- Technology round-ups
- New hires, transfers, promotions, other employee news
- Employee profiles
- Customer profiles
- Customer news
- Community relations activities
- Interviews
- Letters column
- Financial report
- Announcements and write-ups of conferences, seminars, meetings, trade shows
- Photos with captions (of people, plants, and products)
- Announcements of newly published literature
- President's letter
- Sales round-up

All stories should be concise, lively, and interesting, and all should have news or informational value.

The newsletter does not have to be written from scratch. You can use it to recycle press releases, excerpts from executive speeches, published articles, and papers. Lengthy material that the reader might not normally sit through can be condensed and rewritten to make it more readable.

The newsletter can be published as often as you like—every month, every other month, twice a year. But don't publish an issue if you have nothing new to say; it is better to postpone an issue until there is real news to report. The reader will forgive a late issue but will not continue to read a newsletter that publishes nothing of real value. The ideal frequency of publication is quarterly, four times a year. The ideal length is four pages.

Producing your newsletter on your PC using a page layout or word processing program is the simplest and least expensive method of production. If you use a desktop publishing service, an optical scanner can be used to scan in photos for purposes of positioning. In that way the service can provide a proof that is very close to camera-ready.

Informational Booklets

Producing a piece of literature that is wholly or in part informational rather than promotional is an effective tool for building a good relationship with your customers and prospects. People hunger for information—about being a better consumer, managing money, health, career, family, success, love, home, technology. You can win people over by providing some of this much-needed information in your literature.

One tactic is to include some useful information in literature that otherwise makes a direct sales pitch. A product brochure on a line of cosmetics, for example, can contain one page on "How to Apply Makeup." This single page of beauty tips can compel many people to keep a brochure they might otherwise throw away.

Another approach is to publish purely informational literature as part of your total literature program. A seed company, for example, could publish a series of informational pamphlets on gardening as a supplement to its seed catalog. Each pamphlet tells the reader how to grow a certain type of plant. The pamphlets contain no direct sales pitch or production information. But to grow the plant you need seeds—seeds that you can order from the company's catalog.

Let's say you want to publish an informational pamphlet. Here's an outline that you can apply to any topic:

- *Front cover*—Has a title that describes the content of the brochure in a way that highlights its usefulness to the reader. Examples: "Six Ways to Improve Home Insulation," "How to Cut Your Utility Bill by Up to 40 Percent," "A Quick and Easy Guide to Window and Door Weatherstripping."

- *Introduction*—The introduction presents a short discussion of the problem, explains how the advice in the pamphlet can help solve it, and tells the reader how best to use the tips presented. It can also explain the company's motivation in publishing the information (which might be as a service to customers, to ensure proper use of the firm's product, or to educate the public about applications of the product).

- *Body*—The bulk of the copy presents the information, advice, and tips. The best way to present the information is as a series of numbered sections. You should offer the reader anywhere from 5 to 15 tips; less seems insubstantial and more is too much for the reader to grasp.

- *Tables*—If you present a lot of related information, you might help the reader by summing it up in one or two concise tables after the main section of body copy.

- *Wrap-up*—Sums up what the reader has learned.

- *Sales pitch*—Although the informational pamphlet should be free from hype, it's okay to mention your products in one or two sentences at the end. Simply say that you have products available and invite the reader to call or write for additional information. Don't forget to include your address and phone number.

Order Forms

If your products can be ordered directly from your catalog or brochure, you want to make it easy to order by including an order form and a business reply envelope so that the customer can mail his or her order without the expense of postage. Your local post office can tell you how to obtain a business reply permit and produce your own envelopes. Be sure to follow post office instructions; otherwise, the post office may not be able to process and deliver your envelopes.

The order form is a sheet the customer can fill in to order the desired merchandise. The simpler the order form, the more orders you'll receive. A confusing or complicated order form will turn customers off. Here is what you should include on your order form:

- Instructions telling the customer to print or type (handwritten orders can be hard to read).
- Space for customer to fill in name, address, and phone number. Ask for a street address (United Parcel Service and Federal Express do not deliver to box numbers).
- A request for change of address information.
- Space to fill in shipping address if different from billing address (for merchandise ordered as a gift).
- Space for customer to indicate desired mechandise, including quantity and price.
- Instructions on method of payment.
- Credit cards accepted; minimum amount for credit card orders.
- Number the customer can call to order by phone.
- Guarantee.
- Return policy.
- Offer of specials, discounts, and impulse items for sale directly on the order form.
- Information on packing, shipping, and delivery.
- Information on shipping and handling costs and sales tax.
- Thank-you to the buyer for ordering.
- Request the names and addresses of friends who would like to receive the catalog or brochure.
- Question as to whether the customer objects to you giving her or his name to other companies for mail solicitations.
- Code number (so you know which brochure or catalog generated the order).

Keep the order form simple. Don't confuse customers with an overly elaborate order form. Number each step to aid the reader in completing the form. Give clear instructions for completing every step.

Leave enough room for the customer to fill in the desired information. It's frustrating to try to cram in your name and address in a quarter-inch space.

Don't hide the order form. Make sure it's easy to find. Make the order form as large as the catalog or brochure page; otherwise, it can get lost among the pages.

Reply Cards and Fax-Backs

A reply card is an abbreviated version of the order form. Whereas the order form solicits complete information and an order, the reply card is a response device the reader can use to say, "Yes, I'm interested. Please send more information or get in touch with me by phone."

Reply cards are postcards. They can require the reader to add a stamp or they can be "business reply cards" that require no postage. (Your post office can provide you with complete details on how to get a permit for business reply and produce your own business reply cards.)

The front of the reply card contains either a business-reply permit number or a place for the reader to place the stamp. It is addressed to you, so that when the customer drops it in the mail, you'll receive it.

The back of the card has space for the reader to fill in his name, organization, title, address, and phone number. You can also add boxes to be checked off or space in which to answer a few simple questions.

The reply card has two basic missions. First, it allows the reader to take the next step in the buying process. This can be a request for more information, a product demonstration, a phone call, a sales visit—whatever method you choose.

The second mission is for you to solicit some information about potential customers. You can ask the reader to tell you his application, when he plans to buy, what products he is currently using, or how much money he can afford to spend. This information allows you to qualify leads and separate non-prospects from serious potential customers. Figure 4.3 shows a typical reply card.

With facsimile machines now commonplace, even in small offices, marketers are encouraging customers and prospects to fax back rather than mail reply cards and order forms; some even design their reply forms deliberately for fax return rather than mail-in.

Such fax-back forms are usually 8½″× 11″, printed on one or two sides of a sheet of paper. They are similar to reply cards except that, with the added space, there is more room for questions and for the prospect to give detailed information about her or his needs.

Figure 4.3 The prospect fills in the back of the reply card, puts a stamp on the front, and drops it in the mail. In a few days the advertiser receives the inquiry and can take appropriate action.

PLEASE SEND ME THE FOLLOWING:

[   ]   FREE fact sheet on technical writing seminar

[   ]   FREE fact sheet on business writing seminar

[   ]   FREE Special Report – "10 Steps to Better Technical Writing"

[   ]   FREE fact sheet on copywriting seminar

Name _____   Title _____

Organization _____   Phone _____

Address _____

City _____   State _____   Zip _____

We are thinking of conducting a writing seminar: [   ] immediately   [   ] next 6 months
[   ] next 6 to 12 months   [   ] no immediate plans

PLACE
STAMP
HERE

Bob Bly
22 East Quackenbush Avenue
3rd Floor
Dumont, NJ 07628

Do not make the reply form overly complicated or difficult to fill out, even if it is an 8½″ × 11″ fax-back and not a 4″ × 9″ reply card. If the form is confusing or time-consuming, people won't return it.

Figure 4.4 shows a typical fax-back form. Note the simplicity of the design. The fax-back should be in black type printed on white or other light-colored stock; dark-colored paper may not fax clearly. Visuals should be kept to a minimum or not used at all; if used, they should be simple line-art; halftones do not fax clearly.

Figure 4.4 The fax-back form is an 8½" × 11" sheet that is completed by the prospect and faxed back to the advertiser.

Bob Bly's
Business-to-Business
Marketing Communications Audit

In today's economy, it pays to make every marketing communication count.

This simple audit is designed to help you identify your most pressing marketing communications challenges—and to find ways to solve problems, communicate with your target markets more effectively, and get better results from every dollar spent on advertising and promotion.

Step One: Identify Your Areas of Need

Check all items that are of concern to you right now:

- ❏ Creating a marketing or advertising plan
- ❏ Generating more inquiries from my print advertising
- ❏ Improving overall effectiveness and persuasiveness of print ads
- ❏ Determining which vertical industries or narrow target markets to pursue
- ❏ How to effectively market and promote our product or service on a limited advertising budget to these target audiences
- ❏ Producing effective sales brochures, catalogs, and other marketing literature
- ❏ How to get good case histories and user stories written and published
- ❏ Getting articles by company personnel written and published in industry trade journals
- ❏ Getting editors to write about our company, product, or activities
- ❏ Getting more editors to run our press releases
- ❏ Planning and implementing a direct mail campaign or program
- ❏ Increasing direct mail response rates
- ❏ Generating low-cost but qualified leads using postcard decks
- ❏ How to make all our marketing communications more responsive and accountable
- ❏ Designing, writing, and producing a company newsletter

- ❏ Creating an effective company or capabilities brochure
- ❏ Developing strategies for responding to and following up on inquiries
- ❏ Creating effective inquiry fulfillment packages
- ❏ Producing and using a video or audio tape to promote our product or service
- ❏ Writing and publishing a book, booklet, or special report that can be used to promote our company or product
- ❏ Choosing an appropriate premium or advertising specialty as a customer giveaway
- ❏ Getting reviews and critiques of existing or in-progress copy for ads, mailings, brochures, and other promotions
- ❏ How to promote our product or service using free or paid seminars
- ❏ How to market our product or organization by having our people speak or present papers at conventions, trade shows, meetings, and other industry events
- ❏ Training our staff with an in-house seminar in:

  _____
  (indicate topic)

- ❏ Learning proven strategies for marketing our product or service in a recession or soft economy
- ❏ Other (describe): _____
  _____
  _____

Figure 4.4 Continued.

Marketing Communications Audit

Step Two: Provide a Rough Indication of Your Budget

Amount of money you are prepared to commit to the solution of the problems checked off on page one of this form:

❏ under $500   ❏ under $1,000   ❏ under $2,500
❏ under $5,000   ❏ other:

Step Three: Fill in Your Name, Address, and Phone Number Below

Name _____ Title _____

Company _____ Phone _____

Address _____

City _____ State _____ Zip _____

Step Four: Mail or Fax Your Completed Form Today

Mall: Bob Bly, 22 E. Quackenbush Ave., Dumont, NJ 07628
FAX: (201) 385-1220
Phone: (201) 385-1138

If you wish, send me your current ads, brochures, mailing pieces, press releases, and any other material that will give me a good idea of the products or services you are responsible for promoting. I will review your audit and materials and provide a free 20-minute consultation by telephone with specific recommendations on how to solve your marketing problems, implement programs, and effectively address your key areas of concern. To schedule a specific date and time for your free, no-obligation phone consultation, indicate your preferred date and time below:

Preferred date and time _____
Alternate date and time _____

Mail your audit form today. There's no cost. And no obligation.

**Bob Bly ▪ Copywriter/Consultant ▪ 22 E. Quackenbush Avenue
Dumont, NJ 07628**

CHAPTER FIVE

SELLING YOUR COMPANY AND YOUR PRODUCT: THE COPY

Once the copy outline is approved, the next steps are to write a first draft of the copy and to do a rough layout. These are often done simultaneously, so you, the client, can get an idea of how the copy lays out as you read it.

If you are more of a word person than a picture person, you might want to have the copy written first, then go to design and layout once the text is approved. If you are more of a visual thinker, you might have the artist do an initial layout based on the outline, then have the copywriter write text to fit this layout. It's entirely up to you.

Although layouts are usually done by artists, most copywriters like to have some say in the visual appearance of the brochure. If the visual treatment is simple, the writer may include a list of suggested visuals with the copy.

If the layout is complex, or the text is heavily dependent upon layouts and visuals, the writer may submit his or her own rough sketch of what the finished piece should look like. A rough layout drawn by the writer is called a *copywriter's rough*, shown in Figures 5.1 and 5.2.

The copywriter's rough is not a finished layout. It is a guide that shows you and the artist the relationship between the text, the visuals, and their positions on the pages. The graphic artist, using this crude sketch as a starting point, produces a fairly polished rendering of the layout of the piece.

The Interplay of Layout and Copy

The layout serves as a framework for the copy. The designer's job is to make the printed page attractive, to draw the reader's eye to the text, to make the brochure flow smoothly from page to page, and to make the copy easy and pleasant to read.

Figure 5.1   Layout of pages for an eight-page brochure.

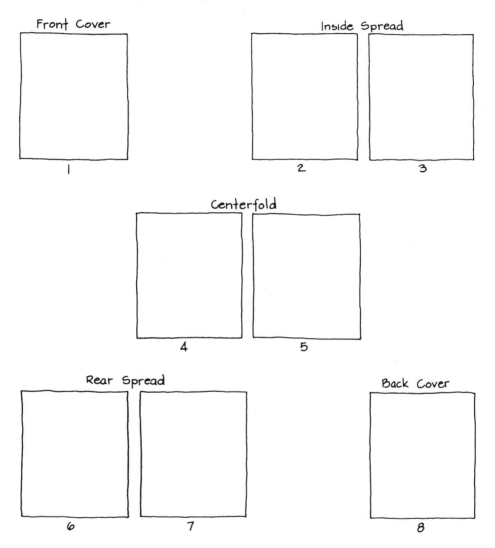

The layout should therefore be designed to accommodate and enhance the copy. The copywriter dictates the length of each section, the number of words in headlines and subheads, the ordering of sections of text, and the total length of the brochure. The artist designs the brochure around the copy.

If you take the opposite view—that design comes first—you'll be in trouble. You'll find yourself force-fitting copy to accommodate an existing design. You'll be cutting and condensing and expanding copy to fit a page layout, when in fact it is the copy—not the layout of the pages—that the reader is interested in.

Figure 5.2   Copywriter's rough for eight-page brochure.

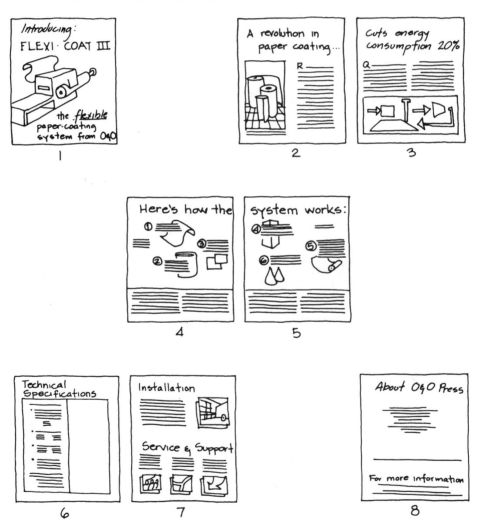

Getting Ready to Write

Whether you, someone else in your organization, or an outside writer is to write the copy, you need to gather the source material that will provide the writer with the necessary background information to produce a first-rate manuscript.

Here's a checklist of the specific types of materials you should gather for the writer:

- Ad reprints
- Brochures
- Annual reports
- Catalogs
- Article reprints
- Technical papers
- Text of speeches and presentations
- Film, videotape, and slide-show scripts
- Press releases
- Market research
- Marketing plans
- Sales reports
- Letters from customers
- Back issues of your company newsletter
- Competitors' ads and brochures

Some organizations say that because their product or service is new, they have no previously published material to give the writer. But this is nonsense. The birth of any new idea or product is accompanied by mounds of paperwork you can give to the writer. This includes:

- Internal letters
- Letters to customers
- Product specifications
- Manufacturer's literature
- Blueprints
- Plans
- Illustrations
- Photos of prototypes
- Engineering drawings

- "White papers" and other internal bulletins
- Instruction manuals
- Marketing plans
- Reports
- Proposals
- Results of laboratory tests and field tests

This is enough to get the writer started. If you want to do even more, you might circle or underline passages in the material that relate to the project at hand. This step is optional, but it can save the writer the trouble of plowing through a lengthy report in which only one or two paragraphs are relevant.

Research

Often the information provided by the client to the writer is incomplete. Key facts are missing and research is needed to get this information before you can complete an accurate first draft.

The *interview* is the basic research tool of the copywriter. The easiest, most efficient way to interview is for the writer to call the client and say, "I have a list of questions about the XYZ brochure. Where can I get the answers?" You, as the client, will have no trouble providing them. Perhaps some of the questions are best answered by sending the writer additional material you didn't think of including in your original package. Other questions can be answered quickly and easily over the phone.

For those questions that you can't answer—because they're too technical or deal with a subject outside your own expertise—you can either get the answers from other people in your organization or have the writer contact these people directly. However, if you ask the writer to call others in your organization, be sure to give these folks advanced warning. Otherwise, they may not be willing to give away company secrets to a stranger over the telephone.

Studying the source material and asking questions should give you or your writer all the information needed to write the copy. But there are a few additional research techniques that can add to your understanding and appreciation of the product, concept, or organization you are trying to promote.

Direct observation is another useful research technique, and it's one that is likely to reveal falsehoods or exaggerations in the research you've done so far. For example, the shop foreman may tell you, "Stress quality control in the brochure. I run the best manufacturing line in the business." When you visit the manufacturing plant, however, you observe old, rusting assembly lines, sloppy workmanship, and a large number of defects rolling off the conveyor belt.

From direct observation you learn that your quality controls are not what they should be. Steps should be taken to correct this but, in the meantime, quality control is not something you want to highlight in your brochure.

Experimentation can also give you additional insights into the product. Now, I know you're not a laboratory scientist, and I don't expect you to run the product through a battery of tests. But a few simple, do-it-yourself experiments can tell you a lot about a product and its key selling features.

For example, a copywriter was trying to come up with an idea for an ad on corn flakes. His client's corn flakes looked the same as other corn flakes; when he poured two bowls and tried them, he found they tasted the same, as well. But minutes later, he discovered that the competitor's flakes had turned soggy in the milk, while his client's flakes stayed crisp. He had found his competitive advantage, and the theme of flakes that "stay crisp in milk" became the basis for a successful ad campaign.

Another research technique at the writer's disposal is to go to secondary sources to uncover additional facts about a product, business, or market. For example, if assigned to write a brochure about a piece of chemical equipment, you might first turn to *Perry's Handbook of Chemical Engineering* and read any articles on this type of equipment. In the same way, if given the task of writing a flier to promote a vitamin mix containing vitamins A, C, and E, you might consult medical reference books to find out the individual properties and benefits of these vitamins.

Secondary-source research isn't a necessity, because your organization is the best source of information about its products. But you may have omitted or forgotten about a fact that can be the basis of a convincing selling argument. Digging into other sources can help you uncover these hidden features.

"Roughing it"

Remember the copywriter's rough? Well, not only is it helpful to the designer, but it can aid the writer in getting her or his thoughts organized.

Any piece of printed literature is broken down into a fixed number of pages. When the brochure is closed, we see only one page, either the front or the back cover. When it's open, we see a number of pages at a time (depending on the way it's folded). This grouping of pages is called a *spread*.

As readers turn the pages, the eye and mind take in the words and layout one spread at a time. In a regular eight-page brochure (Figure 5.1), the reader sees the front cover first. Next is the opening spread, consisting of the inside front cover and the facing page (pages 2 and 3). Next comes the centerfold (pages 4 and 5). Then the spread consisting of page 6 and page 7, the inside back cover. The end of the brochure is the outside back cover.

When writing your copy, think about how the various sections flow from one page or spread to the next. If you have a large table of specifications too wide to fit on one page, you can put it on a two-page spread (say, the centerfold) but you shouldn't break it up by making the reader turn the page to get to the second half of the table.

Use the copywriter's rough to plan the order and layout of the copy. The rough can be a sketch, or, if you prefer, you can construct a *dummy*, a full-size paper model of how the finished piece will look. Figure 5.2 is a sample sketch of a copywriter's rough for an eight-page brochure. Figure 5.3 gives you a blank form you can use to produce copywriter's roughs for a variety of different promotional pieces.

The key to designing a copywriter's rough is to group similar topics on one page or spread. As readers turn the pages they should see (and read) a logical progression of ideas from point A to point B to point C.

Keep in mind that the copywriter's rough is just an aid to the writer, not a final layout. When you get into the writing, you may discover that a section of copy has to be expanded from one page to two, or that the guarantee should go on the back cover instead of on page 6. Go ahead and write it that way, then make the changes on the rough you submit to the artist. But don't let a design dictate the length and direction of your copy; rather, the layout should be changed to accommodate the text.

Figure 5.3 Use this form to create your own rough layouts for a variety of promotions, including brochures, direct mail, and print ads. Copy the form on your office copier, then you can save the original, to copy for future projects.

Copywriter's Rough Layout for:_____

(project)

[   ] **Outer Envelope:**

( ) **No. 10**   ( ) **6" x 9"**   ( ) **9" x 12"**

[   ] **Letter:**   (Page Size:_____ Number of Pages: _____)

Page 1   Page 2   Page 3   Page 4

[   ] **Circular:**   (Page Size:_____ Number of Pages: _____

Format: _____)

Page 1   Page 2   Page 3   Page 4

(Continued)

Figure 5.3   Continued.

[   ] Reply Card: (Size: _____ **)**

```
┌─────────────────────┐   ┌─────────────────────┐
│                     │   │                     │
│                     │   │                     │
│                     │   │                     │
│                     │   │                     │
└─────────────────────┘   └─────────────────────┘
        Front                      Back
```

[   ] Reply Envelope: (Size: _____ **)**

```
┌─────────────────────┐   ┌─────────────────────┐
│                     │   │                     │
│                     │   │                     │
│                     │   │                     │
│                     │   │                     │
└─────────────────────┘   └─────────────────────┘
        Front                      Back
```

[   ] Order Form (Page Size: _____ **Number of Pages** _____ **)**

```
┌─────────────┐   ┌─────────────┐
│             │   │             │
│             │   │             │
│             │   │             │
│             │   │             │
│             │   │             │
└─────────────┘   └─────────────┘
```

[   ] Space Advertisement (Page Size: _____ **)**

```
┌─────────────┐   ┌─────────────┐
│             │   │             │
│             │   │             │
│             │   │             │
│             │   │             │
│             │   │             │
└─────────────┘   └─────────────┘
```

[   ] Other Materials:

If you are writing the copy yourself...

If you're writing the copy yourself and you've never written promotional copy before you might be feeling some anxiety about getting started. Here is some advice that can help:

■ **Don't be overwhelmed**

The tendency is to say, "I'm not a brochure writer. How am I going to do this?" But you've written many other things: reports, memos, letters to friends and family. And that didn't scare you. Neither should writing a brochure. Don't think of it as advertising. Think of it as a letter to a friend. The friend is your customer, and the letter's goal is to convince your friend to try a great new product or service, which just happens to be your product or service. You can even go so far as to write the first draft in letter form, beginning with "Dear Fred" and ending with "Sincerely, Jack." You can always go back and add headings, subheads, and visuals later. Which brings us to the next bit of advice:

■ **You don't have to get it right the first time**

Professional writers don't expect their first draft to be a masterpiece. They know that the essence of writing is rewriting, and that it takes many revisions to produce a publishable piece of prose.

Novices, unaware of this fact, feel they have just one shot, that if it doesn't come out right the first time, they've failed. They agonize over every word they put on the page, and become so nervous that they "block" themselves and become unable to write.

You don't have to get it right the first time. In fact, you shouldn't even try. Your first draft can be as rough and sloppy as you like. You can put down anything that comes to mind. Some nonwriters even prefer to dictate their thoughts into a tape recorder and have a secretary transcribe the tape. Use any method you please as long as you get *something* down on paper.

■ **Edit**

Once you've got some material on paper, the next step is to revise the copy. Read the text and change it to make it better. Delete words and sentences that are unnecessary or repetitive; add more material where the copy seems insubstantial. Reorganize paragraphs and sections into a more logical order. Add descriptive headlines and subheads. Break out some material into sidebars and tables, and indicate where photos or drawings can help illustrate a point. Add connecting phrases to smooth the transition between sentences and paragraphs.

Next, polish your copy. Once it is in reasonable shape, edit further to make it sound even better and more persuasive. Read carefully the words you've written. See if using a different word or phrase can improve what you've written. Read the copy aloud to make sure it flows smoothly and contains no awkward passages. If it doesn't read smoothly, fix it. Check grammar, punctuation, and spelling. Also review for accuracy, consistency, and completeness of information.

■ Sleep on it

As I've said, a good writer rewrites copy many times before considering it finished. One way to make this rewriting process more productive is to put each version aside for an evening and look at it with fresh eyes the next morning. Refreshed, you are able to review your copy more objectively and spot mistakes you might have missed when you were fatigued. If you have the time, put the final draft aside for a few days and review it once more before sending it to the designer. You'll probably spot opportunities for improvements you didn't see before.

■ Do the easy parts first

I've already mentioned that breaking the copy into sections makes the brochure easier to read and easier to write. Most novice writers feel compelled to write the brochure in order, and so they begin with the introduction and work their way through to the back cover. But it doesn't have to be done this way.

In fact, if you have a tough time getting started, I recommend that you start with the simple sections first: the list of branch offices, the table of technical specifications, the physical description of the product, the corporate biography. Once you get a few sections down on paper your "writing momentum" will build and you'll get enough steam up to run right through the entire job.

10 Tips on Writing Good Copy

The goal of the brochure writer is to get the message across and have the desired influence on the reader. Promotional literature doesn't strive for strict grammatical accuracy or the scholarliness of a Ph.D. thesis. The copywriter instead aims for a friendly tone, clarity of expression, persuasiveness, and content that is complete, informative, and accurate. Here are 10 tips to help you achieve these goals:

1. Start selling on the cover

Whether the reader gets your literature in the mail or plucks it off a rack, the first thing seen is the cover. The message on the cover either compels the reader to turn the page or dampens the reader's interest, in which case the brochure is discarded and forgotten.

Even so, the majority of advertisers waste the front cover. They decorate it with the product name, a fancy graphic, and the company logo, and hope that their initials and symbol are enough to prod the reader to go on. But they are not.

The cover should contain a strong selling message, usually stated in the form of a headline. This message can contain a product benefit, highlight the usefulness of the product (or of the brochure itself), identify the audience the brochure is aimed at or the applications the product is designed for, or stress how the product saves time, money, and aggravation. You can see how by applying a little thought and imagination to the problem, the choice of cover headline increases the selling power of the piece. Take, for example, the headline on a pamphlet promoting a bank's Christmas club:

> IMAGINE HAVING
> AN EXTRA
> $520
> FOR THE
> HOLIDAYS.
>
> It's easy.
> It's painless.
> It's automatic.
> It's just $10 a week.

This headline is more likely to grab the depositor's attention than a pamphlet labeled, "Christmas Club Account."

A headline isn't the only way you can begin your sales pitch on the cover. Another way might be to tell a story with one or more dramatic photographs. A booklet used in a fundraising mailing for the Humane Society might feature dramatic photos of mistreated animals.

2. Make your story flow

A brochure is in many ways a miniature book and, like a good book, a good brochure tells a story. The story has a beginning, a middle, and an ending and flows smoothly from one point to the next.

Once you've written the first draft, sit back and read it as you would an article or short story. Does it progress logically? Or are there points where the transitions are awkward, where you are jarred by a phrase or sentence that doesn't seem to belong?

If the transitions are clumsy, they'll need to be smoothed. Perhaps the material needs to be rearranged a bit. Maybe an extra subhead or headline or an introductory paragraph will take care of the problem. Or perhaps a transitional phrase can bridge the gap between one sentence and the next. Here are some of the transitional words and phrases that copywriters use to make a sensible connection between one sentence and the next:

> Additionally,…
> Also,…
> And,…
> Another reason is…
> As a result,…
> …as well as…
> As we've discussed…
> At the same time,…
> Best of all,…
> But,…
> But wait. There's more…
> By comparison,…
> Chances are…
> Even better,…
> Even worse,…
> First, (_____). Second, (_____). Third,…
> For example,…
> For instance,…
> Here's how:
> Here's why:
> However,…

If (_____), then...
Imagine:
Most important,
Importantly
In addition,...
In other words,...
In this way,...
Moreover,...
Most important,...
Obviously,...
Of course,...
On the other hand,...
Or...
Perhaps...
Plus,...
Remember:
Similarly,...
Since...
Still,...
That's where (_____) can help
Then again,...
The results?...
Therefore,...
There's more:
Thus,...
To be sure,...
What's more,...
Why? Because...
Yet,...

3. Strive for a personal tone

When writing promotional literature—or direct mail, a letter to a customer, or any other business communication—write in a natural, relaxed, friendly style. I don't mean that you should be chatty, or sound like a yokel, or throw in a lot of *you knows*, *yeahs*, *wows*, and other slang. Written language has to be more precise, more concise than speech.

But you *should* strive for the easy, conversational tone of spoken language—the short words, the short sentences, the personal touch. Friendly copy bespeaks a friendly organization: an organization that people will want to do business with.

John Louis DeGaetani of Harvard Business School has devised a simple test for ensuring that your copy is conversational. "As you revise, ask yourself if you would ever say to your reader what you are writing," instructs John. "Or imagine yourself speaking to the person instead of writing." If what you've written sounds stiff, unnatural, or dull, it's not conversational and you need to revise it.

4.   Stress benefits, not features

When you are enthusiastic about your job, your work becomes a major part of your life. As a result, your view of what you and your organization do becomes somewhat distorted. You believe the world centers around your business or cause when, in fact, it doesn't. You believe people are fascinated by every detail of your product when, in fact, their only concern is what the product can do for them.

Too many promotional brochures stress the *features* of the product or service—the bare facts about how it works, what it looks like, how it is made, where it is made, who designed it, and so on.

Effective copy translates features into benefits. A benefit is a reason why the customer should buy the product. A benefit explains what the product can do for the customer. It tells how the customer can come out ahead by doing business with you: how he or she can save money, improve health, do a better job, protect her or his family, save time, earn more money, gain status, feel good about her- or himself, enjoy life.

The easiest way to uncover the benefits of a product is to examine it first-hand (or read the source material) and list its features on the left side of a sheet of paper. Then, in the right-hand column, write down one benefit of each feature. Here's a partial list I came up with for a handy, familiar item—my clock-radio:

Feature:	Benefit:
Large illuminated digital display	Time easy to see at a glance— even at night.
Snooze alarm switch	Tired? Just hit a button for 10 more minutes of sleep.
Digital alarm set	Wake at precisely the moment you want to.
Wood veneer finish	Handsome design fits in with your bedroom decor.
Felt pads on bottom	Won't scratch or smudge furniture.
Alarm/radio option	Wake to the sound that suits you— gentle strings, hard rock, or the buzz of an alarm.
AM/FM	Clear reception guaranteed. Gets *all* your favorite stations.

You get the idea. You don't want to settle for telling the reader what the product is. You want to tell him what the product can do for him. Copywriter Luther Brock says that effective promotional copy places "100 percent emphasis on how the reader will come out ahead by doing business with you."

5. Be specific

Specificity is the heart of good writing, and that includes brochure writing.

Many brochure writers use an elegant style of copy, full of fancy phrases and dramatic statements, but short on facts. They fear that facts will bore the reader, so they strive for drama, entertainment, and literary style.

The fact is that people read brochures because they want information. And they are quickly turned off by brochures that are long on puffery but empty on content. "Platitudes and generalities roll off the human understanding like water from a duck," wrote Claude Hopkins in his book, *Scientific Advertising*. "They leave no impression whatever." Specifics, on the other hand, stick in the mind. They are remembered. And they sell.

Be specific. Don't write, "low, low prices" when you can say "50 percent off all carpets in stock through Sunday." Don't say "we're reliable" if you can tell the customer, "The repairman arrives within 24 hours or we fix it free of charge." Don't be content to talk about "a lot of energy saved" if you know your insulation "reduces heating bills by 30 to 50 percent a month." Remember, specifics sell.

6. Support your claims

There is one problem, though. Even if you stress benefits instead of features, even if you make specific claims, the customer still may not believe you. In his book *Direct Mail Copy That Sells*, copywriter Herschell Gordon Lewis describes modern times as an Age of Skepticism:

> This is the Age in which nobody believes anybody, in which claims of superiority are challenged just because they're claims, in which consumers express surprise when something they buy actually performs the way it was advertised to perform.

How can you overcome skepticism and get people to believe you? Here are some things to include in your brochure:

Guarantees.   Offer a guarantee: money back, free replacement, unlimited service, work redone at no cost. Guarantees allow the customer to try the product at no risk and ensure satisfaction. The message they carry to the consumer is, "This product must work; otherwise, the manufacturer wouldn't guarantee it." A guarantee is the most powerful tool for overcoming skepticism. If the guarantee is a strong one, or if it is unusual to offer a guarantee on your type of product, you might stress the guarantee as a major selling point in your copy.

Letter from the president.   Many catalogs include a "personal" letter from the company president to the consumer. In the letter, the president stresses the firm's reputation, the quality of its products, its dedication to service, and its promise to keep the customer satisfied.

People like to deal with the person in charge; this is why you so often hear a dissatisfied customer tell a clerk or waiter, "Let me speak with the manager, please." When the chief executive of an organization speaks, it leaves more of an impression than words from an anonymous copywriter.

Testimonials.   A testimonial is a statement of praise or endorsement from a satisfied customer (or, in some cases, a celebrity). The testimonial is written in the customer's own words, appears in quotation marks, and is usually attributed to a specific person.

The person's affiliation, title, or city of residence is included, if appropriate. If the person doesn't want her or his name used, you can comply by using initials and address only ("Here's what E.G. in Florida says about…"), but the full name is better for overcoming skepticism. The quotation can range in length from a sentence to a few paragraphs. It's always more impressive to include several testimonials rather than just one, but one is better than none.

Case histories.   Case histories can be published as separate bulletins, or you can include one or more case histories in condensed form within the text of a brochure. Case histories tell the customer, "When we talk about our service, we're not just being theoretical. Our product works in the real world. Here's proof!"

Trials.   Some things have to be seen to be believed. So let the customer see your product and use it for a trial period.

Traditional mail-order companies—especially magazine and book publishers—use this technique with success. To get you to subscribe to a magazine, they offer to send you the first issue free. If you don't like the magazine, you keep the free issue and cancel your subscription without payment or penalty. Or, when you order a book by mail, the publisher sends you the book on a 15-day free trial basis. you read the book and, if you don't like it, you send it back—again, without paying for it.

Now more modern industries are adopting this technique. Take software, for example. No matter how detailed the brochure, the customer can't really appreciate the benefits of the software without sitting down at the computer and using it. So companies selling programs that cost hundreds of dollars will offer to send customers a condensed version of the program (known as a *demo*) first. The customer gets the demo free or for a nominal sum. Once he sees how good the demo is, he can feel confident ordering the $395 program by mail.

Personal demonstrations.   Some products can be demonstrated only in person, either by a salesperson or a qualified technician. In your brochure copy, you state that you can prove your claims with a live product demonstration in the customer's home or office or at your place. Then urge the prospect to contact you to arrange this demonstration.

Test results. Has your product proven its superior performance in tests? If so, include the test results in your copy. The best tests for overcoming consumer skepticism are those performed by an impartial third party, such as *Good Housekeeping* or *Consumer Reports*. But be aware that some of these organizations (*Consumer Reports*, for example) do not allow manufacturers to include their test results in advertising and promotional literature. The second-best tests are field tests: the product performing successfully in an actual customer installation. Third-best are tests you perform in your own research laboratories.

If what you say in the copy is likely to raise questions in the consumer's mind, you must put this reader at ease by answering these questions in that same piece of copy.

For example, I know a ghostwriter (a person who writes novels, plays, articles, books, and stories that are published under his clients' by-lines). Many people would hesitate to hire him because of his policy of full payment in advance. So he devotes one section of his pamphlet to explaining the reasons for this policy, reasons which, when you read them, seem perfectly logical and reasonable. By explaining the reasoning behind this policy, the pamphlet generates considerable business for the ghostwriter.

Following are some ways to convince prospective customers that you mean what you say:

Stress your good track record. Consumers are distrustful of new, unproven products and small, fly-by-night operations that are here today but gone tomorrow. If you buy a new roof with a 20-year guarantee, you want to buy from the company that's going to be around to honor the guarantee, not the independent contractor who may decide to quit tomorrow and retire to Florida.

Prove to the consumer your stability and reputation by talking about your track record and past successes. Cite number of years in the business, number of employees, the size of your operation, number of warehouses, number of plants, number of offices, annual sales, profits, reputation. Talk about what you've done, who you've done it for, and how successful you've been. This builds the reader's trust in you.

Demonstrate the product in print.   The next-best thing to offering an in-person demonstration is to demonstrate the product in print. For example, a flier claims a new four-step dental procedure to be quicker and easier than the conventional method. The flier shows a series of photos and captions to demonstrate the new procedure, step by step. You can use the same technique to demonstrate many products: a blender, a do-it-yourself home repair kit, a tool, a dishwasher, a boiler.

Show, don't tell.   Don't just say your product or service saves money or improves life. Show that it does. Say you're selling an energy-efficient air conditioner. Instead of just talking in a general sense about energy savings, provide sample calculations that show *exactly* how much money buyers can save based on their utility rates, room size, BTU rating, and thermostat setting. Make it easy for the reader to follow the calculation and come up with money saved based on his specific situation.

Compare yourself with the competition.   If your product or service clearly beats the competition, you can include comparisons. Be sure all claims of superiority can be substantiated by fact; if in doubt, leave it out.

Unless your comparison is completely factual and can be supported by documentation (i.e., specifications taken from competitors' brochures), don't identify the competition by name. Some advertisers play it safe by putting product comparisons in a separate bulletin. If a competitor threatens a lawsuit or changes its product in response to your comparative advertising, you can stop using the comparison sheet while continuing to circulate your in brochure.

Figure 5.4 shows an ad that compares a software product to its competitors without naming those competitors. Using this type of checklist comparison is very effective, because the superiority of your product becomes evident the product in print. For example, a flier claims a new 4-step dental procedure to be quicker and easier than the conventional method. The flier shows a series of photos and captions to demonstrate the new procedure, step by step. You can use the same technique to demonstrate many products: a blender, a do-it-yourself home repair kit, a tool, a dishwasher, a boiler.

Figure 5.4 An excellent way to show the superiority of your product versus the competition's is to create a checklist pointing out the features you have that they do not.

Now YOU can control changes and revisions on software development projects...

...at **half the cost** of conventional configuration management systems

Managing the changes and revisions on large software development projects can be a file-keeping nightmare.

MKS RCS is the solution.

MKS RCS (Revision Control System) enables you to record a complete history of your project's development...**control** the changes and revisions...and retrieve any version on command—at about HALF the cost of other systems.

MKS RCS: the price/performance leader in configuration management software
Available on DOS, OS/2, and 386 UNIX, MKS RCS costs 40 to 60 percent **LESS** than what our major competitor charges. And, as a multiple-license MKS RCS user, you get a **full year** of the best tech support in the industry...plus the next upgrade... **at no extra cost.**

Get the facts—FREE.
Call or write us today for a free brochure and 30-day free Evaluation Copy of MKS RCS. No cost or obligation of any kind.

35 King Street North, Waterloo
Ontario, Canada N2J 2W9

Call toll-free 800-265-2797 (U.S. & Canada)
or (519) 884-2251 • Fax: (519) 884-8861

MKS and MKS RCS are trademarks of Mortice Kern Systems Inc.
UNIX is a registered trademark of UNIX System Laboratories, Inc.

Compare yourself to alternative solutions.   Many products and services have two types of competitors: direct competitors (similar products and services offered by other firms) and alternative solutions to the same application. For example, a word-processor manufacturer's direct competitors may include IBM, Compaq, and Apple. But he also has to sell the word processor as the best solution for achieving more productive writing as opposed to such alternative solutions as electric typewriters, electronic typewriters, hiring a secretary, outside typing services. If your prospects are using conventional products, show how your innovative approach is better, faster, and more economical.

7. **Keep the copy lively**
Here are a few tricks of the copywriting trade to help keep your copy lively:

Vary sentence length.   Most copywriting texts tell you to keep sentences short, because short sentences are easier to read. But writing gets monotonous when all sentences are the same length. So vary sentence length. Every so often, put in a fairly long sentence. Also use an occasional very short sentence or sentence fragment. Like this one.

Use personal pronouns.   Lively writing is personal, not impersonal. Personal pronouns (*we, they, us, you*) make the copy sound less lawyerlike, more like person-to-person conversation. Addressing the reader directly as *you* in the copy adds warmth and creates the illusion in the reader's mind that the copy was specifically written just for her or him.

Provide news.   Thousands of people who would never read a novel or a poem relax in the evening with the daily paper. Why? Because people are interested in what's new. If you can include news in your copy—about a product, a service, a company, an industry, a program, a technology, or a community—do so. It makes copy more lively.

Tell stories.   Human beings have been telling and recording stories since the first caveman drew a crude picture of his latest hunting experience on the cave wall. Story-telling is an inherently powerful technique for getting your message across, much more so than a dry recitation of mere facts.
You can use story-telling to liven up your promotional copy. For example, instead of just stating that your bottle-coating process is superior, tell how one

of your customers actually doubled his bottling business because of your better coating.

Include people.   People have a great interest in other people. You can add interest to your copy by referring to people, real or fictitious.

Let's say you are describing a new procedure for employees to follow when making medical claims. Instead of writing "the employee should" or "the employee shall," create an employee and outline the procedure in story form: "Doris, a parts inspector, was feeling overly tired and wanted to get a checkup. First, Doris took her orange form A-12 to Personnel. Next,…" You get the idea.

Also, when taking photos of a product, manufacturing plant, office, or building, put people in the photos to add interest. (Putting a person in a product shot also provides a comparison of scale that shows the reader how big or small the product is.)

Use short paragraphs.   Long blocks of copy tire readers out. Keep paragraphs and sections short. It makes copy easier to read (and easier to write).

Use heads and subheads.   Use plenty of headlines and subheads to break up the text. Make the heads and subheads descriptive ("coating system prevents fuming problems"), not just functional ("coating system"). The reader should be able to get the gist of your sales pitch by scanning the heads and subheads without even reading the body copy.

Separate and highlight key information.   In many pieces of promotional literature, the copy is split between an exciting sales message and a boring recitation of dull but necessary descriptive facts and specifications.

Don't let your exciting message get bogged down with dull details. If you have a list of technical specifications, for example, put them in a separate table or sidebar, and keep your body copy lively. (A sidebar is a short article or section of copy separated from the main text and enclosed in a box or other graphic device.)

Think visually.   Photos, charts, drawings, and diagrams can go a long way toward adding interest to your text. If something is better communicated with a visual than with words, use the visual.

8. Make sure the information is relevant

All copy should be interesting to read, but not everything that's interesting to read belongs in your copy.

Copy should be relevant to the message you're trying to communicate. If it is irrelevant, it may entertain, but the promotional literature won't communicate the message you want it to. And the people you really want to reach—the ones that are likely to buy your product, join your club, take your course, or donate to your cause—are likely to be turned off by copy that fails to get to the point.

For example: a brochure selling heavy-duty and industrial batteries begins with a two-page essay on the history of batteries, ranging from ancient Egypt to the Voltaic Pile to the invention of the lead storage battery. Sounds interesting, you say. Yes, to a history buff. But the industrial engineer looking for specific information on battery size and performance may not be willing to wade through this unnecessary verbiage to get to the size, price, and performance information.

9. Check the accuracy

Then check it again. Then have three or four other people in your organization check it, too. A single mistake can result in the need to reprint the entire brochure. And that's expensive. So even though proofreading is boring, it's well worth the time and effort.

In addition to accuracy, you should also check for consistency. Make sure you've used the same style of grammar, punctuation, capitalization, spelling, numerals, abbreviations, titles, and product names throughout the copy. If you're inconsistent—if you write "GAF" in some places and "G.A.F." in others—you're automatically wrong part of the time.

10. Don't forget the details

One manufacturer spent $2,400 revising and reprinting its product sheets only to discover that the company's phone number had been omitted on the new sheets!

We devote so much time and energy to the promotional aspect of our literature that we sometimes tend to shrug off the details. But these details can be just as important as your sales pitch and graphic image.

Review your copy before it goes to the designer. Make sure you have included the following:

- Logo
- Company name
- Address
- Phone number
- Fax number
- Extensions
- Toll-free number
- Store locations
- Directions
- Hours
- Credit cards accepted
- Branch offices
- Telex and TWX
- Guarantee
- Disclaimers
- Other required legal wording
- Brochure date and code number
- Permissions and acknowledgments
- Trademarks and registrations marks
- Copyright notice

The lack of this so-called fine print can kill the effectiveness of an otherwise fine promotion. For example, one restaurant handed out hundreds of promotional fliers offering a substantial savings on a fine dinner at their grand opening. The flier was widely distributed but brought in little business. Why? Because the restaurant was in a hard-to-find location, and although the flier contained the address, it didn't give directions, and potential customers couldn't find the place.

Fitting the Copy to the Rough

Once the copy is finished, you may want to go back to your copywriter's rough—the crude sketch of the layout—to see how your completed copy compares with your original plan. Perhaps some sections have been moved and others deleted. Or maybe you've written more copy for the application section but less for the introduction than you planned. Chances are your finished manuscript isn't exactly what you indicated on the copywriter's rough, so you may want to redraw the rough based on the final copy. Or you can give your copy and copywriter's rough to your graphic designer, and have her or him do a more polished comp (drawing of the layout).

As this is done, you can produce a more exact version, because you now know how long each section of copy is. Take a look at this new layout. Does it leave more room for illustrations than you thought? If it does, go back and reread the copy. Are there additional visuals you want to include in your brochure, pictures and drawings that can help get your message across even better? If so, indicate them on your layout and your manuscript.

On the other hand, you might have more copy and less room for drawings. If so, consider whether all of your proposed visuals are really necessary. Perhaps some of the borderline ones—visuals you like but don't really need—can be deleted. Or, you can redo the layout to accommodate them.

The Copy Review Process

If you're the boss in your organization, you have the final say on what copy is acceptable and what is not. But if you're not the head honcho, you probably have to get others to read and approve the copy before you can release it to the printer. Here's how to go about it.

If the brochure is mostly text and has a simple layout, you can get approval on copy only. If the layout contains a lot of visuals and the copy depends on the visuals and layout, give the unapproved copy to the designer first, have the designer do a layout, as just described, and then submit the copy and layout for review together.

Attach a "copy review sheet" (Figure 5.5) to the manuscript and circulate it to the reviewers. The sheet lists the reviewers in the order they are to receive and review the manuscript. Review starts with the person of least authority and ends with the person who has final say.

You send the copy to the first reviewer. He or she reads the copy, makes any changes, initials the sheet, and passes it on to the next reviewer. The last reviewer to read the manuscript returns it to you.

Reviewers are people in your organization who are involved with the product or service described in the proposed brochure and therefore have a say in what the finished piece should contain. You may also want to get the opinions of some people not directly involved: sales representatives, consul-

Figure 5.5   Attach a copy of this form to your manuscript and circulate it to the appropriate people.

Dear Reviewer:

Please read carefully the attached draft of our organization's new promotional literature.

You may mark specific comments, corrections, and suggestions directly on the copy, or attach a separate sheet if needed.

When you complete your review, initial next to your name below. Pass this on to the next reviewer by the date indicated.

The last reviewer should return the manuscript to _____

_____ by _____ .

Thanks for your cooperation.

NAME   INITIALS   REVIEW BY:

_____

_____

_____

_____

_____

_____

_____

_____

Note: If you have any questions please call me at extension _____.

tants, distributors, engineers, and others who may be knowledgeable and have something to contribute.

Send these people a copy along with a cover memo that says, "Enclosed is the copy for a forthcoming brochure on _____. I'd like to get your comments and criticisms on this copy. If you have suggestions on how to improve this copy, may I hear from you by _____(date)_____?"

Although you are asking these people to comment, it is for their opinions only, not approval. You are obliged to make the changes requested by your boss, but you can choose either to heed or to ignore the advice passed on by people who are not official reviewers.

Although it takes a little prodding and reminding people, you'll eventually get your manuscript back with changes and comments. If the changes are minor and specific, retyping may be all that's needed to produce a finished, approved manuscript. But if the revisions are extensive, the writer may have to take the reviewed copy and make the requested changes.

Don't send the writer's revised draft through this one-at-a-time review process again. Instead, send a copy to all reviewers at once with a cover memo saying, "Here is the revised manuscript for the _____ brochure. It contains all changes and revisions requested. If you have any comments or additional changes, please give me a call or send a marked-up manuscript to me by _____(date)_____."

This allows reviewers to get a last look and give the copy their final blessing. Otherwise, some irate executive may complain bitterly that you ignored her suggestion when, in fact, you didn't.

CHAPTER SIX

FINDING YOUR LOOK: THE DESIGN

As discussed in Chapter 3, there are many places to turn to for design services: ad agencies, PR firms, marketing communications companies, art and copy services, design studios, free-lance graphic artists. All of these are qualified to handle the job for you. The question is: Do you need their help? Or can you do the job yourself? The answer depends on the complexity of the task at hand and the level of quality you seek.

Simple pieces—fliers, sales letters, typewritten newsletters, folded pamphlets—can often be done cost-effectively in-house using a desktop publishing system. Such a system consists of a personal computer, a laser printer, and appropriate word processing and desktop publishing software.

The computer can be a Macintosh or an IBM PC or compatible. The graphics and publishing industries tend to use Macintosh, whereas most of corporate America seems to be equipped with IBM PCs running MS-D0S, 0S/2, or Windows. You can use either Macintosh or IBM for desktop publishing, because disks can be converted from Macintosh to IBM format and vice versa.

Consult your local PC dealer or consumer magazines on personal computers for guidance on the most appropriate or popular desktop publishing software for page layout and illustration.

Some printers can take your disk and the copywriter's rough layout and set the copy into type for you for a nominal fee. Most printers have also switched to typesetting on the Macintosh.

But if the promotional material is sophisticated, then the design of the page, the use of color, the selection of type, the treatment of visuals, and the arrangement of elements on the page are crucial and complex. Here's where you need the graphic designer, because you probably don't have the skill or the experience to plan a design on your own.

Using professionals gives your piece the professional touch, and that's really what you want. Remember, owning a desktop publishing system doesn't make you a professional artist any more than owning an expensive set of golf clubs makes you Arnold Palmer. Saving money by doing the layout yourself makes sense on low-level and simple projects where the costly skills of a graphic designer are neither needed nor warranted. But in my experience most amateurs and desktop publishing users think their sense of design is better than it really is. So it may pay for you to hire a professional.

Sure, hiring artists can be expensive. But the quality—and hence, the effectiveness—of your print promotions goes way up.

You should also weigh the cost of hiring the artist against what your own time is worth per hour and how long it would take you or an employee to do the job. A competent desktop publisher can be hired for $25 to $50 an hour, can do the job faster than you can, and frees you to concentrate on more profitable tasks.

Selecting the Right Designer

The most important factor in choosing an artist is *style*.

Every graphic artist has an individual style. Some artists, for example, produce very slick, modern graphics. Some are almost abstract or surrealistic in their approach. Others produce plain-Jane graphics with clean, crisp, highly readable type and layouts. Others use lots of warm colors and folksy artwork for a homey, Norman Rockwell–type look.

Chances are, you already know the image you want your literature to convey. And you have a pretty good idea of how your literature's graphic look should fit that image. Be sure, then, to choose an artist whose style is in sync with your own. If you want a homespun image for your mail-order catalog, choose the Norman Rockwell–type artist, not the abstract painter or the high-tech, futuristic designer. But if you're selling satellites, the futuristic look may be just the thing for you.

Don't make the mistake of choosing a designer and then trying to force that person to change her or his style to fit the look you want. It won't work. Artists can't (and shouldn't be expected to) switch styles any more than you can switch your personality. Choose an artist in whose work you see a reflection of the way you'd like your own literature to look.

The second most important factor in choosing a designer is attitude. To ensure that the design is completed to your liking and on time, choose a designer who brings a businesslike attitude to the job.

Here are some other factors to consider when hiring a graphic artist:

Portfolio. Carefully examine the artist's portfolio of sample work. Do you like what you see? Would you feel comfortable having your own literature done in this artist's style? Or is it too far-out or fancy or dull for you? Does the portfolio contain samples of published work similar to the job at hand? Or does the artist lack experience in your area, be it brochures or catalogs or annual reports? Pick an artist whose style and specialty mesh with your own.

Clients. Ask to see a list of clients. Does the artist have an impressive client list? Has he worked for clients in fields similar to your own? Call some of the clients on the list. Were they pleased with the artist's work? How did they like dealing with the artist—was he or she a pleasure or a pain to work with? One warning: A graphic artist unable to produce a client list is probably a beginner without much experience in commercial graphics.

Capabilities. Make sure the artist has the resources to handle your type of assignment. If you're producing a highly technical brochure, pick an artist who is comfortable working with complicated graphs and other technical illustrations. If you're producing a full-color catalog, make sure the artist knows how to prepare work for a color press.

Systems. Many clients today look for graphic artists who use equipment compatible with theirs. If all of your work is done on a Macintosh using Quark, you might prefer to work with an artist who can give you the finished artwork on a disk in Quark, enabling you to load it onto your system and make refinements and changes on your Mac without going back to the artist each time.

Price. Find out how you'll be charged for the job: by the hour, by the day, or by the project. What is the artist's best estimate for the job? What if there are changes, how much will they cost? Will you be billed on completion of the assignment or in stages? Will the artist put a mark-up on typography and other outside services and products he or she buys for you? That last question is important. You may want to avoid the mark-up by buying type, paper stock, and other outside products and services directly.

The more specific you can be about the job, the more precise the artist's estimate of the cost will be. When you meet with a graphic artist to discuss the job and get an estimate, present your copywriter's rough, the current draft of your brochure text, and the literature specification sheet you completed (see Chapter 2). This material will make it easier for the artist to give a firm price quotation.

Ability to meet a deadline.   Tell the artist your deadline and ask whether it can be met. Some designers are in great demand and are booked many months in advance. Others have studios full of assistants and work round the clock to meet the tightest deadlines. Don't pressure an artist into rushing to meet an impossible deadline. Instead, choose a designer who is comfortable working within your time constraints.

Professionalism.   Choose a graphic designer who blends skill, taste, and style with a businesslike attitude, a professional manner, and a respect for budgets, deadlines, and the limitations that the commercial nature of your project places on the designer's artistic freedom. Don't choose an artist who views your brochure as an opportunity to create a work of art at your expense; choose one who wants to create a brochure that works for you.

Working with the Designer

You've hired a designer. Now what? Does the designer go home and send you a finished brochure and a bill two months later? Or do you sit at the designer's side day and night, supervising the positioning of each word of type, each square inch of artwork?

The process of working with a designer falls somewhere between these two extremes. The designer does most of the creative work independently, working at a studio away from your office and watchful eye. The two of you do get together at various stages of the project to review the work and make sure the direction it takes is to your liking.

This is basically a five-step process:

Initial consultation

The project begins with a briefing. You sit down with the designer to explain your goals and the type of finished piece you're looking for. Discussing design is more difficult than talking about the copy, because it's difficult to describe, in words, the images you have in your mind. Here's how to go about it: Give the designer the current draft of the brochure text. If it's final, approved copy—great! The designer can go directly to setting type. If it's a rough draft, say so. The designer won't set type, but can still use the manuscript as a guide to the length of each section and of the brochure as a whole.

The designer should also receive your copywriter's rough. This drawing shows the designer which visuals go with which sections of text and how the copy and art might be divided on a page-by-page basis. Be sure to explain that the rough is just that—a guideline only—and that the designer should feel free to use it, improve it, or discard it altogether if he can come up with something better.

There are two additional tools you can use to communicate your ideas to designers. These are *sample files* and *circle layouts*.

The sample file is a file of the literature you've collected, literature that you sent for by mail or picked up in stores and at trade shows. Before starting any literature project, go through your sample file. Pick out any samples with graphic techniques or styles you think might look good in your own work. Then, when you meet with your designer, you can point to a sample to show exactly what you're talking about. For example, if you like a particular typeface, show your artist a brochure that uses this style of type. If you like an unusual paper stock, show a brochure printed on this stock. Build a sample file so you can precisely communicate your likes and dislikes to the artist.

In the circle layout, a technique described by Lewis Kornfeld in his book *To Catch a Mouse, Make a Noise Like a Cheese*, you draw rough shapes—circles, ovals, squares, rectangles—to show the approximate position and amount of space each element of your layout (headline, subhead, body copy, picture, logo, charts, etc.) should take on the printed page. The logic of this technique is that you, the client, dictate the importance of the various components of your message, which is how it should be. The designer can judge from an aesthetic point of view, but the layout should emphasize visuals and text from a promotional point of view, and no one knows the value of your message better than you do.

The advantage of this technique is that it requires no artistic skill. Anyone who can lift a pencil can, in less than a minute, create a circle layout. Figure 6.1 shows some samples.

Figure 6.1 Circle layouts provide a quick and easy way of showing the relative importance of the various elements in a page layout. And no artistic skill is required to create them.

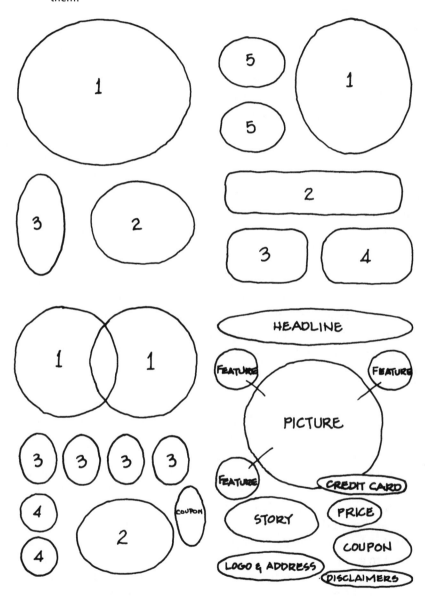

Of course, you are free to use all or none of these techniques. How much guidance or freedom you want to give your designer is up to you. Communicating your needs and preferences as precisely as possible is an excellent way to work with designers, but make it clear that what you are really interested in is getting the best design possible, not just a dressed-up carbon copy of your own primitive layout. (If you say this, mean it. Don't tell the artist, "Feel free to *create*!" and then, when you get the layout, say, "Why didn't you draw it the way I told you to?") A good client is clear about her or his requirements but open to new ideas.

Thumbnails

After the initial briefing, the artist goes back to the studio to work on your project. You can do your bit by letting the work proceed in peace. Don't badger the artist with daily visits or calls to see how it's going. It's going fine. The artist is a professional and can do the job without your supervision.

You and the artist meet again to review the work done so far. At this meeting, the artist will show you some thumbnails. Thumbnails are miniature sketches about the size of wallet-size photos, done quickly and designed to give a rough idea of the general look and feel of a design. They lack detail and are meant to show overall direction only. Don't be put off by their crude appearance; they aren't supposed to have a finished look.

If the designer is relatively certain of the direction the design should take, you will see only one set of thumbnails representing one design concept. Or, the designer may show you several sets of thumbnails, representing two, three, or even four different concepts. The designer will probably recommend one favorite concept and present the others as alternate choices.

Why thumbnails? Why not just go to the finished layout? Because the nearer to completion the project, the more it costs to make revisions and changes. (Keep this in mind, because it applies to all phases of literature production.) Thumbnails don't take the artist much time to produce, so this step allows changes to be made rather inexpensively. If the literature were already typeset and pasted up, changes would be extremely costly.

Study the thumbnails. If you like what you see, give the artist your approval to go on to the next step. If you like the basic concept but want some changes, discuss them with the designer. Ask for an opinion on whether the changes would weaken or improve the piece. Sometimes, the designer will agree with your suggestions. In other cases, you may find disagreement. Listen to the advice you get from your designer without assuming that you always know what's best. After all, when it comes to layouts, your artist is the pro.

When viewing a series of thumbnails, you might pick one version and then find that your artist prefers another version. Discuss the reasons for the artist's preference. You may find yourself agreeing.

If you don't like anything you see, don't say "this stinks" or "I don't like any of this" or "you've done a bad job." Instead, explain exactly *why* you aren't satisfied with the layout and give specific suggestions as to how it can be changed to suit your liking. When you criticize the work of outside suppliers, your comments should always be constructive, specific, and stated in a manner that won't insult or offend the person. This is a key principle of brochure production, and it applies to every phase of the job.

If all the thumbnails totally displease you, you will ask the artist to go back to the drawing board and submit a new set. But if you approve the thumbnails as is or with modification, the next step is to look at an artist's rough.

Roughs

A rough is an artist's full-size sketch of the layout of each page of the brochure. It shows the position and size of headlines, subheads, body copy, pictures, colors and tints, borders, tables, charts, graphs, drawings, sidebars, footnotes, and any other text or visual elements.

Headlines and subheads are written on the artist's roughs so you can quickly determine the subject matter of each page or spread. Body copy is usually represented by a series of straight or squiggly lines since the actual type won't be set until layout and copy are approved. Some designers working with desktop publishing systems will include actual text in the rough layout because the computer makes it so easy to make changes.

When you look at an artist's rough, you get a good sense of what the finished piece will look like, and this can be a revelation. A graphic technique that sounded questionable when the artist described it suddenly looks great on the page. Perhaps you discover that the table you crammed onto page 3 really would look better spread across the centerfold. Or maybe the copy is longer than you thought and needs some subheads to break it up.

Together, you and the artist review the rough and fine-tune the design. With the rough in front of you, design is no longer an abstract concept—it's real. You can see how each suggested change affects the overall appearance.

Comprehensives

The comprehensive, or "comp," is a tighter rendering of the rough layout. It is as close to the finished piece as a drawing can be. If you made changes on the rough, the comp will give you a chance to see these changes before the piece is typeset and pasted up. If top management must approve copy and layout, a comp makes it easier for them to visualize the printed piece.

Even at this stage, changes can still be made at reasonable cost. Remember, a comp is just a sketch. Type has probably not been set, no photos have been taken, no illustrations rendered. That's why going through these steps is worthwhile, it allows you to change your mind without paying a fortune to do so.

Traditionally, roughs were crude and comps finely rendered; and both were done by hand. With desktop publishing and page layout software, roughs and comps are frequently done on the computer, making it easy to change and revise the layout. When the copy is written and stored on disk, the artist can easily include copy in the rough or comp, and today there is often little distinction between these two steps or stages.

Dummies

Making a "dummy" of the proposed literature is also a worthwhile step. A dummy is a full-scale model of the brochure. It is constructed out of the paper stock selected for the brochure, and is folded or bound in the same way the finished piece will be.

The dummy gives you an idea of the look, weight, and feel of the brochure, as well as the flow (how smoothly the story unfolds as you turn from one page to the next). As with the rough, holding a dummy in your hands can be a revelation. The lightweight paper you thought was fine when you picked it from the printer's sample book looks cheap and flimsy when stapled into a booklet. Perhaps you need to give the booklet more weight by printing the cover in a heavier stock. Or you may find that your glossy colored stock picks up fingerprint smudges when handled. A different color or coating would solve that problem.

It's especially important to create a dummy when the brochure is to be mailed. There are two reasons for this.

First, you can weigh the dummy and find out the mailing cost based on this weight. You may discover that going to a slightly lighter weight stock significantly reduces the required postage. Second, you should make sure the dummy fits into a standard envelope. If it doesn't, you'll need to print a custom envelope, and that's expensive.

Also, the post office has regulations concerning the size of envelopes, and not all sizes and shapes are acceptable. If your proposed brochure is oversized or oddly shaped, check with the post office to make sure it will be acceptable for mailing, and get this clearance in writing. Otherwise, you may spend thousands on your unique booklet only to discover that the post office refuses to mail it.

Design Considerations

Here are some design factors you'll have to make decisions about, along with some tips on making the right selection.

Page decisions

■ Number of pages

The number of pages is a function of the length of the copy, the number of visuals required, and the amount of copy and visuals per page.

The copy dictates the size of the printed piece. Obviously, a 3,000-word brochure needs more pages than a 300-word brochure. However, by writing concisely and eliminating unnecessary words, you can cut down the length of the text and, hence, the number of pages. This type of editing also saves money, because printing costs increase as a function of the number of pages and typesetting costs increase as a function of the number of words.

Editing also applies to visuals. Use them if they enhance and clarify your message, but don't include a picture just because you like it. Each picture adds to the total cost of the job.

Some designers, striving for an elegant, understated look, use a lot of white (blank) space on each page. The result is often striking, but it increases the page count and the associated printing costs.

Try not to spread your layout too thin. You—and many professional designers—would be surprised to learn how much copy you can put on a page and still make it attractive, eye-catching, and readable.

■ Page size

The choice of page size depends, in part, on how you distribute your literature and how your customer makes use of it.

If you can design your brochure to fit in a standard business envelope (known as a number 10 envelope), mailing costs will be lower than for a full-size brochure that must be mailed in a 9″ × 12″ envelope.

Literature that will be displayed at exhibits or in retail outlets should be designed to fit standard display racks. Travel agents, for example, use racks for pocket-size (4″ × 9″) brochures; full-size literature may not fit.

Pocket-size guides are handy if you want the reader to be able to carry the literature (for example, a pamphlet on gas-saving tips should fit in an automobile glove compartment). But you should use full-size pages (8½″ × 11″) for materials that people are likely to keep. These pages fit neatly into a standard file; a larger brochure may stand out from the crowd, but risks being thrown away because it is too long to fit in the file; a small pocket-size brochure can get lost in a file.

If the reader is a purchasing agent or someone else who might store your literature in a three-ring binder, be sure to leave margins so the three-hole punch doesn't interfere with text or graphics.

Layout also plays a part in choosing a page size. Literature with many sections of very short copy is best suited to a pocket-size folder with six or eight panels; each panel can contain one or two sections of copy. A technical bulletin with large graphs, charts, and tables requires larger pages for adequate display of the material.

■ Page format

Most brochures are laid out with either two or three columns of type per page (see Figure 6.2). Many designers prefer the three-column format because of its greater flexibility in laying out the page.

In the three-column layout, visuals can be one, two, or three columns wide. Most visuals should be two columns wide to maximize the size of photos and illustrations while leaving sufficient room for accompanying text.

Type decisions

■ Type style

How do you choose a typeface? First, look for readability. Above all else, the type must be easy to read and inviting to the eye. After all, the message you want to communicate is contained in the text, if people don't read the copy, your efforts are wasted.

Figure 6.2   Brochures are generally designed witht text running in two or three columns. Two-column layouts have wider columns of type and avoid the small spot illustrations and photos that sometimes appear in three-column layouts.

WHAT IS THE CENTER FOR TECHNICAL COMMUNICATION?

The Center for Technical Communication (CTC) is a company that specializes in improving the writing skills of corporate employees and the quality of written communications within your organization.

CTC's primary service is conducting in-house workshops in technical and business writing for corporate clients nationwide. Our on-site writing seminars give your employees the skills and confidence to write better, faster, and more productively.

CTC also offers public seminars, conferences, and publications covering all aspects of technical and business communication. Other services designed to improve the quality of communication in your organization include our telephone hotline, fax critique service, contract technical writing services, and more.

INHOUSE WRITING WORKSHOPS

CTC offers the following in-house training seminars for corporations and associations:

Effective Technical Writing

A 1 or 2-day workshop on how to write clear, correct, technically accurate reports, manuals, documentation, specs, proposals, papers, and other technical documents. This program is designed to improve the writing skills of engineers, scientists, systems analysts, technicians, technical writers, technical editors, and others whose writing deals with technical or semitechnical subject matter.

Effective Business Writing

A 1 or 2-day workshop on how to write clear, concise, persuasive letters, memos, reports, proposals, and other business documents. This program's focus is on improving the writing skills of executives, managers, professionals, and support staff.

Our instructors know technical writing because they are technicians and technical writers.

What sets CTC apart from other training firms is that our instructors are not only skilled and entertaining trainers but are also *recognized authorities in* their fields. Our technical writing seminars, for example, are taught by instructors who hold technical degrees, have worked as full-time professional technical writers for large corporations, and have taught technical writing at the university level. In-depth experience and technical background not only improve the quality of instruction but also break down barriers between the instructor and the audience: Your technical trainees become more receptive when they realize the instructor is a "techie" like them.

PUBLIC SEMINARS AND CONFERENCES

Although CTC gives priority to meeting the in-house training needs of our corporate clients, we occasionally sponsor public seminars and conferences on technical and business writing. Companies with six or more people requiring training, however, will probably find an in-house program more cost-effective.

TRAIN-THE-TRAINER PROGRAM

Some companies do not have the budget to send as many of their employees as they'd like through our technical writing workshops. As a cost-effective alternative to on-site training, we offer a train-the-trainer program in which CTC licenses its course materials, including outlines and handouts, to you for use within your organization. We also coach your trainers in how to present our program effectively.

PUBLICATIONS

CTC offers books, special reports, monographs, audio cassettes, handouts, and other training materials on a variety of topics including technical writing, marketing communications, and business communications.

THE TECHNICAL WRITING HOTLINE™

This unique telephone hotline gives you instant access to technical writing experts who can provide immediate answers to questions concerning grammar, punctuation, spelling, usage, word choice, format, and style.

Second, type style has a major effect on the image your literature conveys. Helvetica, for example, has a clean, modern look. Souvenir Medium has a warmer appearance. Eurostile Extended looks futuristic and technical. And Nuptial Script is just right for a wedding invitation.

There are literally thousands of typefaces available today, but an individual printer or graphic designer typically has access to just a few dozen, which makes it somewhat easier to make your selection. Ask your designer to recommend a type and to show you some alternatives in case you don't like his first choice. You may even want to sit down with his type book (a book showing sample typefaces) and see which you like best.

Also, there are many variations in weight (thickness) of the lettering within a family of type. Helvetica, for example, includes Helvetica Light, Helvetica Medium, and Helvetica Bold, plus italic versions of each of these. You could set body copy in medium, headlines in bold, footnotes and other fine print in light.

In general, it's best to stay with one family of type per brochure and avoid mixing typefaces within a single piece. Resist the temptation to use lots of different fonts and type families simply because you have them on your desktop system.

■ Type size

This one's easier. Type is measured in points. The body copy in promotional literature should be set in 10- or 12-point type; in no case should type be smaller than 9 point. Type size of headlines and subheads depends on their length, but they are usually set several sizes larger than the body copy to make them stand out.

■ Use of headlines and subheads

Used as a design element, headlines and subheads help pull the reader's eye through the body copy. In addition, well-written, descriptive heads and subheads allow readers to skim the brochure without reading the entire text and still get the gist of the story. In laying out the page, the artist may discover that the writer has not used enough subheads to adequately break up the text. If this is the case, ask your writer to go back and add a few more subheads.

Production decisions

■ Folding versus binding

A folded piece of literature—one in which the pages are formed by folding a single sheet of paper—costs less to print than a booklet made by mechanically binding together several sheets of paper. But a piece of paper can only be folded so many times, so the size of folded brochures is limited. If you need more than 12 pages, you'll have to use staples, glue, or some other mechanical method of binding.

Figure 6.3 shows some of the ways to bind pages. For brochures, the most popular is the saddle-stitch method, in which staples are driven through the spine of the brochure from the outside cover. Take a look at some pieces of literature that cross your desk and notice the position of the staples.

■ Paper stock

The type of paper you choose—its look, color, weight, and texture—has a major effect on the image conveyed by your literature. A fine, textured, uncoated stock has an elegant, dignified look and feel, whereas a paper coated with a reflective metallic surface looks more high-tech.

The best way to select paper is to construct a dummy out of the proposed stock. Then keep the dummy on your desk for a while. Do you like the way it looks? Does it have enough heft to it, or is it too flimsy? Does the paper stand up to repeated handling, or does it tear, crease, or smudge? Black and other dark coated stocks, for example, are notorious for picking up fingerprints when handled.

Some pieces of promotional literature, such as flip-chart presentations, are subject to excess handling and abuse. These should be printed on a heavier stock, such as cover stock or thin cardboard, that can stand up to repeated handling. You can even laminate pages with a thin, transparent plastic for added protection. This might be done in cases in which the literature will be handled in an environment where people have oily or dirty hands, such as for a brochure aimed at gas station mechanics or oil-field workers.

Paper stock, size, and number of pages are the factors that determine the weight of the piece. So if the brochure is to be mailed, using a lighter stock can save on postage costs.

■ Attachments

If your literature is to be distributed with inserts or supplements, you may want to design it with a pocket for holding these extra materials. If the literature is to be mailed with a business card, you can cut slots into a page for insertion of the card. If you want to include cloth swatches or other physical objects with your literature, you might glue these samples to the pages. Any inserts, cards, loose sheets, or three-dimensional objects you intend to attach to your brochure must be planned for by the designer.

Figure 6.3   Of the various binding methods, saddle-stitch is most commonly used for binding promotional brochures. Staples are driven through the spine of the brochure into the centerfold.

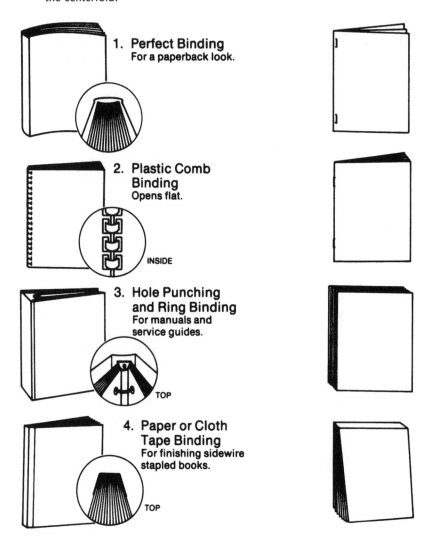

1. **Perfect Binding**
   For a paperback look.

2. **Plastic Comb Binding**
   Opens flat.
   INSIDE

3. **Hole Punching and Ring Binding**
   For manuals and service guides.
   TOP

4. **Paper or Cloth Tape Binding**
   For finishing sidewire stapled books.
   TOP

Figure 6.3   Continued.

5. **Sidewire Binding**
   For scientific reprints or business reports.

9. **Collating and Corner-Stapling**
   For research notes, newsletters and presentations.

6. **Saddlewire Stitching**
   For small booklets and brochures.

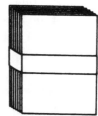

10. **Paper Banding**
    For securing loose pages.

7. **Shrink Packaging**
   For loose pages that require handling or shipping.

11. **Duo-tang**
    For protection for all printed matter. To allow pages to be added at a later date.

8. **Padded Material**
   For memo pads, telephone messages, order forms, and specification sheets.

12. **Tabs**
    Can be added for easy division of categories in most binding processes.

■ Pop-ups, die-cuts, and other gimmicks

There are many gimmicks you can use to make your brochure stand out from the crowd. These include *pop-ups* (three-dimensional paper sculptures that pop up when you open the brochure), *embossing* (a technique that raises lettering or other portions of the design), *die-cuts* (sections cut out of the page), *varnishes* (to add an extra sheen to photos or bands of color), and *special folds*. And there are new gimmicks invented every day. A recent one is an inexpensive microchip that you can paste on the page; the chip plays music when you open the brochure.

Gimmicks must be carefully worked into the design to enhance the look and message of the piece. A gimmick used for its own sake is a waste; it draws attention to itself and away from the sales message. Gimmicks should relate directly to the theme and subject of the brochure. For instance, a booklet promoting a word processing service could use a pop-up of a PC.

Art decisions

■ Number of colors

A *one-color* job is the least expensive and is printed with a single ink. Most one-color jobs are black ink on white paper (newspapers, for example). But a one-color job could use a different color ink, such as blue or brown.

In printer's jargon, the number of colors (one-color, two-color, four-color) refers to the number of different colored inks used, and doesn't take into account the color of the paper. So, by printing a red ink on gray paper, you can create a "one-color job" that has two colors—red and gray.

A *two-color* job uses two inks, and is about 15 to 20 percent more expensive to print than a one-color job. Most two-color jobs print black ink on white paper, with the second ink being blue, red, or yellow. But again, you can be more imaginative.

A *full-color* job uses the four basic printing colors—black, blue, red, and yellow—to reproduce artwork and photos in full, natural color. Full-color can run as much as double the cost (or more) of black-and-white, depending on the number of color photos included.

When deciding on how many colors to use, keep cost in mind. Otherwise, you may not be able to afford to print the brochure you've paid someone to design.

Image also plays a part. Four-color printing conveys an image of quality, size, and wealth. However, a good designer can create this image with two colors and a fine-quality paper stock at much less cost than a four-color job.

If color photographs play a key role in making the sale, use four-color printing on a glossy white paper stock. This gives the best reproduction of your photographs. Color is important in literature promoting food, fashions, home decorating, travel, collectibles, and other products and services sold primarily on their visual appeal.

If, however, the brochure is all copy, one or two colors are adequate for the job.

■ Color scheme

Don't just use color because you think it looks classy. You're paying extra for color, so make the color work to enhance your message or the visual appeal of your layout.

The Red Devil Company, a tool manufacturer, prints every job in black and red; the red is used to highlight their logo, a graphic of the devil. In a recent Bloomingdale's ad featuring a photo of a glamorous woman wearing an expensive necklace, the entire ad was black and white, except the necklace, which appeared in full color. The effect was striking and served to draw attention to the item being sold.

■ Photographs versus drawings

Photos are useful for showing what a product looks like, for demonstrating its performance, and for adding believability. Drawings, on the other hand, are best for showing how something works, how it is put together, and what it looks like inside (where it would be difficult to photograph). Drawings are also useful for visualizing products and projects that are planned but not yet completed, such as a new corporate headquarters or the prototype of a new machine. Chapter 7 covers the use of photographs and drawings in more detail.

■ Amount of text and artwork per page

Do you want to cram as much text and as many visuals on each page as you can? Or do you want the piece to be light on copy and easy on the eye?

This choice depends mainly on your audience. If you're writing for people who read a lot—teachers, for example—it's okay to have a dense, copy-heavy page, as long as the typeface is easy to read and the page neatly laid out. But if you're writing for people who are too busy to read much, or for people who are not readers, cut back on the amount of copy and leave plenty of open space on each page. The space makes the page more inviting to the eye and makes the brochure seem less intimidating.

■ **Cover concept**

The cover can serve several purposes. It can deliver a complete message, get the reader to pick up the brochure and open to page one, create or reinforce a corporate identity that associates the product with its maker, and identify and select an audience by market, industry, application, or other criteria.

The design should be used to achieve the desired goal. For example, a series of brochures describing a family of power tools should have a consistent cover design to build an identity for the product line. This consistency can be achieved in many ways: with a tag line, a style of type, a logo, a graphic device, or even photographs of each tool in a similar setting.

10 Tips for Creating a Good Design

1. Think of the layout as a framework, not as artwork

Some artists think of the layout as an end in itself rather than as the means by which the visuals and copy communicate their message. And that's a mistake. Promotional literature isn't artwork, it's promotion. An aesthetically pleasing layout is a waste if it doesn't present the copy and pictures in an appealing, easy-to-read format.

Unfortunately, there are some graphic artists more interested in winning design awards than winning readers. You can spot them by their layouts, which are full of graphic techniques that look slick but hinder readership of the copy. These techniques include:

- Copy set in bizarre typefaces
- Type printed over a tint or a visual
- Lack of contrast (e.g., black type on dark gray paper)
- Reverse type (white type on black background)
- Type set in all italics
- Type set entirely in upper-case letters
- Overuse of white space
- Type set too small to read
- Pages consisting mainly of color bands, borders, or other design elements
- Several pages left blank or used for graphic effect only
- Use of abstract artwork
- Photos not directly related to the subject of the brochure

This is just a partial list. The point is that the layout is a communications tool, whose sole purpose is to make the brochure inviting and easy to look at and read. A good layout does not call attention to itself; it calls attention to the subject matter of the piece. Stick with layouts that are functional, not fanciful.

2.   Start selling on the cover

If any part of the layout is most subject to randomly applied creativity on the part of designers, it's the cover. But the cover should be used to select an audience, grab its attention, state a strong message, and get the reader to turn the page. It should not be designed as if it were a painting to be hung and admired in an art gallery. Yet many designers design covers just that way.

The cover should feature an attention-getting headline that is clear, simple, and direct. The headline should draw attention by promising a benefit, addressing a problem, or showing readers that the contents of the brochure are relevant to their needs.

3.   Emphasize the important points

It's not enough to cover all the important points in the copy. You've got to highlight key points using graphic devices, such as boldface type, italics, bullets, and subheads. If you don't, your readers may miss these key points. For example, according to an article in *TWA Ambassador*, the Northwestern National Bank in Minneapolis wanted to see whether customers read the fine print in the informational booklets it mailed to customers. So in one booklet, they included an extra paragraph offering a free $10 bill to any depositor who asked for it. However, they buried the paragraph in 4,500 words of technical information. The booklets were mailed to 100 customers. *Not a single customer asked for the free $10.*

A good layout highlights and emphasizes key copy points. Some of the graphic techniques you can use to achieve this emphasis include:

- Underlining key words and phrases
- Setting key words and phrases in italic type or boldface type
- Printing select paragraphs in a colored type
- Surrounding a section of text with a border
- Printing a section of text against a tinted background (keep the tint light to ensure readability)
- Printing copy in capital letters (short phrases only)
- Calling attention to specific sections of copy with arrows, circles, and asterisks

- Setting key points apart as call-outs or bursts (a burst is a star-shaped graphic containing a special message)
- Tables
- Lists with items separated by numbers or bullets
- Copy printed on fold-out flaps or pages
- Copy printed in the margins separate from the main text
- Use of more than one style of type. The second type is used sparingly to highlight select sections of copy.
- Sections of copy separated from each other by lines, color stripes, or other borders.
- Space between paragraphs.

As I've already pointed out, not everyone will read your copy straight through. Some readers will merely flip through the pages and scan the text. Such graphic devices as boldface type, underlines, call-outs, and the other techniques listed above can make key points jump out so the casual reader can get the gist of the story at a glance.

4. Keep it simple

Graphic artists are under constant pressure—both from their own egos and their clients' demands—to continuously come up with innovative layouts that are new and different. Sometimes a clever layout can make a brochure stand out from the crowd, but most of the time the simplest layout is the most effective.

Why? Because our reading habits are formed by books, newspapers, and magazines, and these publications use simple, clean layouts unadorned by fancy graphic tricks and techniques. In fact, a complex layout can reduce a brochure's readership, because readers are uncomfortable with the unconventional.

One common mistake is the use of a series of complicated folds to form a brochure with a nonstandard page layout. Such a piece looks interesting at first glance, but unconventional folds usually inhibit reading, because people are unable to figure out the sequence in which the pages should be unfolded and read. You're better off with a standard layout in which page 2 comes after page 1—less creative, but more effective.

5. Readability comes first

A layout can be many things: slick, neat, colorful, eye-catching, inviting, exciting, dignified—even beautiful. But the designer's first priority should always be making the copy easy to read.

Choose a type style that is highly legible and pleasing to the eye. Experiment with type size until you find the one that's easiest to read. Be sure to choose a type that will reproduce clearly on the printing press. Some types with thin letters won't reproduce heavily enough: other types with thick letters may appear as blotches when certain inks and papers are used. Small and thin typefaces may become illegible when faxed.

Set dark type on a clean, light background. Black lettering on white paper is usually best. Don't obscure type with extra colors and tints, or by printing it over photos or drawings. Use standard layouts, such as two or three columns on an 8½″ × 11″ page. A single column is usually too wide for easy reading.

Don't be afraid to speak up if your designer proposes a layout that achieves an interesting look by sacrificing readability. Such a sacrifice isn't worth it. Remember, people pick up brochures largely for the words they contain. Those words should be easy and enjoyable to read. Never make the reader strain or work to extract your message from a messy layout.

Also, keep in mind that many sales brochures are photocopied and circulated to numerous people within an organization. Brochures printed on dark paper or with oversized pages or complicated folds won't reproduce cleanly on an office copier. They are also difficult to fax.

6. Visuals should make a point

Edit visuals as you edit your copy. Ask yourself, "Does this picture transmit information, tell a story, or prove a point? Or is it just for decoration?" Omit visuals that adorn but don't communicate. Make every picture count.

Here are some visuals that *do* tell a story. You improve your literature by including such illustrations:

- Pictures of the product
- Pictures of product installations
- Pictures of the product in use
- Pictures of people enjoying the benefits of using the product (a family sitting around a warm fireplace in a nice home can illustrate the benefit of properly planning family finances)
- Pictures of manufacturing facilities, research labs, and other operations of your organization
- Tables of applications and uses
- Pictures showing how to use or assemble the product
- Tables of product specifications

- Graphs showing performance, efficiency, and growth
- Pictures of product components or raw materials
- Pictures showing the benefits of using the product
- Pictures of the product package
- Diagrams showing how the product works or how it is put together

7. One visual should dominate the page

As a rule, it's better to have one central photo per page than many small photos. A large color photo of good quality is a real attention-getter and gives the page a focal point (a graphically interesting area that draws the eye to the page).

With many small photos, there's no focal point for the reader's eye to focus on. Also, from a cost point of view, printing one large color photo is much cheaper than printing three or four small ones.

An occasional photo montage can be striking. But, as a rule, your layout should have one central visual dominating each page or spread.

8. Be consistent

The design should he consistent throughout the brochure. If page 2 uses headlines in boldface Helvetica type, then so should pages 3, 4, 5, and 6. Continuity from page to page pulls the many elements of the layout together to form a cohesive design. In the same way, different publications within a series of booklets or brochures should have a similar, family look.

9. Avoid clichés

There are visual clichés that constantly appear in just about every type of promotion. Some of the more popular ones include the wide-eyed administrative assistant staring at the screen of her new computer, the gray-haired team of business executives debating around the conference table, and the hard-hat engineer staring blankly into the camera lens as he gives testimonial to the latest ball bearing or piston pump.

These visuals were fresh once, but now they're tired and overused. Try to think of a new way to get your message across graphically. You'll wake up bored readers and create a lot more interest in what you're trying to say.

10. Don't design over budget

The designer has to work within the limitations of your project budget. The choice of colors, use of visuals, selection of paper stock, and arrangement of pages all have a major effect on the cost of producing and printing the piece.

Be honest with your designer. Present a budget to work within, and let the artist know whether (and by how much) it is flexible. A designer knowledgeable in printing and production techniques will create a layout that can be produced within your budget guidelines.

CHAPTER SEVEN

GETTING THE PICTURE: ILLUSTRATING YOUR PROMOTIONAL LITERATURE

One of the main advantages of brochures, catalogs, and booklets over letters and memos is that promotional literature can be illustrated. You can use photos and drawings to tell a story, transmit information, clarify the text, provide a visual change of pace, build an image, prove a claim, or create a mood.

Properly used, photos and drawings are a powerful sales tool. Terry C. Smith, a communications manager at Westinghouse, outlined some of the advantages of using visuals in his book, *How to Write Better and Faster*:

> People *believe* in illustrations. A diagram of a proposed organization is more "believable" than a word description. When presented in graphic form, rough estimates seem more precise than they really are. An artist's concept of a revolutionary new piece of equipment makes its development seem just over the horizon. And, of course, nothing beats an actual photograph for adding authenticity.

To Illustrate or Not to Illustrate?

You know from your own experience that many, many products simply cannot be sold in print without a picture or drawing. Can you imagine, for example, an ad for a new fashion line that didn't show the clothing? Or how about a brochure on a new car that doesn't include pictures of the auto's roomy interior and stylish exterior? Most product literature is more effective when illustrated.

Of course, there are problems as well as advantages with using photos and artwork. Anne Eisenberg, a teacher and writer, talks about one of these problems in her book *Effective Technical Communication*:

> Illustrations are tricky. They can be so effective that they transcend the text, or so poorly conceived that they cloud the message.
>
> Whether they succeed or fail, however, they do have one thing in common: all are expensive to produce. And therefore most illustrations are subject to the question, Is this illustration window dressing, or will it help the reader?
>
> If all pictures were worth a thousand words, there would be no problem; but this is rarely the case. Instead, illustrations range from the useless to the superb; you...will need to cast a cold eye upon them.

Many clients have told me they believe that "no one reads the copy" but "everyone looks at the pictures"—we should therefore use lots of pictures and keep copy to a minimum.

Pictures indeed attract attention and require no reading. But are they more effective than text at communicating a message? If words are so unimportant, why do most companies agonize over the copy they put in their ads and brochures, going through numerous drafts and levels of approval?

Here's what Rudolph Flesch, author of *The Art of Readable Writing*, has to say about an overreliance on visuals to get across your message:

> The idea that you can explain things without explaining them in words is pure superstition. A favorite proverb of the picture-and-diagram lovers is "One picture is worth a thousand words." It simply isn't so. Try to teach people with a picture and you may find that you need a thousand words to tell them exactly what to look at and why.

The cost factor

As I mentioned in Chapter 3, hiring a photographer for a day's shooting costs $1,000 on average. Commissioning an illustrator to draw a piece of equipment or paint a portrait in full color can run you $500 to $1,200 or more, depending on the complexity of the assignment.

For this reason, the key to illustrating your literature at reasonable cost is *selectivity*. As Anne Eisenberg points out, you must evaluate each proposed photo or drawing and ask yourself, "Does it pull its own weight? Does it enhance the brochure enough to justify the cost?" If it doesn't, take it out, even if you love it. Otherwise, your budget will quickly get out of control.

If selectivity is the number one factor in successfully illustrating your promotional literature, simplicity has to be a close second.

Simple illustrations are the best illustrations. Photos, drawings, and diagrams should not contain too many subjects or be cluttered with unnecessary detail. Photographs should be crisp and clear; drawings clean and uncluttered. Messy, sloppy, "busy" visuals are unappealing to the eye, and people tend to skip over them. A simple visual, one with a striking, clearly defined subject, is what draws the reader's eye to the page.

The 10 Basic Types of Visuals

Visuals used in promotional literature fall into one of 10 basic categories. Here are the categories, along with tips on how each type of visual is used:

1. Drawings

A drawing is used to show what something looks like. Use drawings instead of photos to illustrate subjects that are not easily photographed or that can't be photographed at all. In a booklet on fossil fuels, you may want to get across the idea that fossil fuels are the decomposed remains of dinosaurs. To dramatize this point, you might show a color drawing of a *Brontosaurus* grazing on ferns, or perhaps a *Tyrannosaurus Rex* battling it out with *Triceratops*. You can't photograph these creatures, of course, because they are extinct.

2. Photographs

Like the drawing, the photograph is used to show what something looks like. The difference is that photos make the subject seem more believable, more real. If you are raising funds for a new hospital wing under construction, a prospective donor might say, "Where's the proof that my money is going to such a project?" An architect's drawing of the proposed wing can help convince the reader that the project is real. But a photo of the girders going up offers irrefutable proof.

3. Maps

A map shows where something is located. The most common use of maps in promotional literature is to impress the reader by showing the number of man-ufacturing plants, branch offices, sales reps, warehouses, and other facilities you have. Let's say you have 43 offices worldwide. Just saying "we have 43 offices" may not make much of an impression. But showing the offices as 43 red dots on a map of the world immediately communicates the scope of your operation. In many cases, visuals can have much more of an impact than words.

Another use of maps is to show connections between things and places. A map marked with a series of criss-cross lines could be used to show the routes covered by an airline, the pipelines of an oil company, or perhaps the phone lines linking a telecommunications network.

4. Schematic diagrams

A schematic diagram (See Figure 7.1) is a detailed drawing of the interior or exterior of a product, system, or process. It is used to show how the product, sys-tem, or process works.

Let's say you want to explain the operation of a trash disposal unit installed in the kitchen sink. You could draw a picture of the unit with parts cut away to show the interior. Call-outs (captions with lines pointing to vari-ous sections of the diagram) explain how it works, step by step. If the explanatory text is too long for call-outs, you simply number the diagram at various points; these numbers correspond to a series of numbered paragraphs in the main portion of your text.

5. Exploded views

An exploded view is a drawing of a machine or other product with its compo-nent parts *exploded* or pulled away from the center. This shows how the machine is put together. If you've ever looked at the instruction sheet for a plastic model car or plane kit, you've seen an exploded view.

Exploded views are most often used in the operating or assembly instruc-tions for stereo cabinets, bicycles, food processors, desks, and other products that you put together or assemble yourself.

6. Block diagrams

A block diagram consists of a series of boxes linked by connecting lines. The lines indicate the relationships between the boxes, and boxes are labeled to represent people, places, products, or other items in a family of related items. They can also be used to show the steps in a process, such as to illustrate how steel is manufactured or how a machine performs a multistep task.

Figure 7.1   This schematic diagram with call-outs highlights the rugged construction of the hazleton submersible pump.

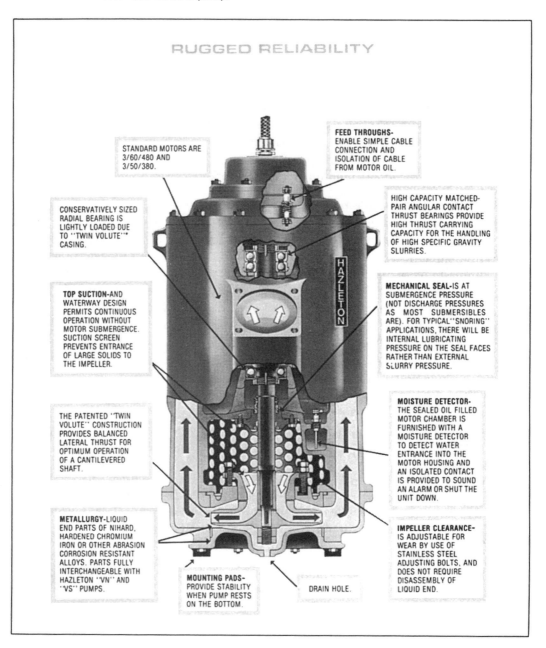

The block diagram is also used to show how a family, association, plan, or system is organized. The familiar "family tree" used to trace a family's origin is an example of a block diagram.

In promotional literature, block diagrams are most frequently used to depict the organization of a corporation or the ranking of its chief officers. The top box, for example, could represent the chairman of the board. The box underneath would represent the chief executive officer, and underneath her or him is the president. A line coming out of the bottom of the president's box branches off into several boxes, each representing the vice president of a different division or functional area (manufacturing, operations, finance, research, marketing). Lines coming out of these boxes go to officers lower in the hierarchy: division managers, branch managers, supervisors, and so on.

7. Graphs

A graph consists of a curve or series of curves framed by horizontal and vertical axes. (The horizontal is known as the x axis and the vertical as the y axis.) Graphs are used to show how one value varies as the function of another value. A table of numbers can also show this, but the graph dramatically highlights trends in visual form. For example, a graph showing how your electric bill increases for each degree you lower the setting on your air conditioner paints a more dramatic picture of costs than merely listing or describing the numbers in the text.

One effective way to use graphs is to highlight data on the performance of a product: fuel efficiency, product life, storage capacity, power consumption. Graphs are also handy for helping the reader size and select a product. If you're selling an expensive industrial boiler and want to give the reader a quick, rough estimate of what it will cost, you could show a graph of cost as a function of boiler size. Calculations in the text tell the reader how to pick the proper boiler size; the graph provides a quick fix on what that particular boiler will cost.

8. Pie charts

A pie chart is a circle that, like a pie, is cut into slices. The pie chart is used to show proportions and percentages. The slices are cut and sized according to the percentage of the total that each slice represents (See Figure 7.2). To achieve clear visual separation between slices, artists often make each slice a different color or shade. Let's say you sell VCRs and want to compare your share of the market with your competitors' shares. If you have 25 percent of

Figure 7.2   (a) Pie chart showing percentage of market share. (b) Exploded pie chart with slice pulled away to highlight market share of company "A."

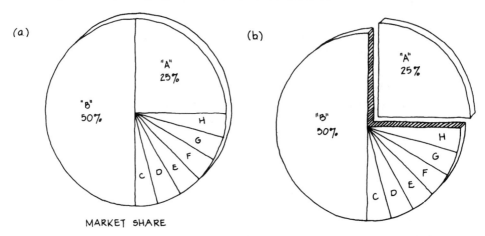

MARKET SHARE

the market, your slice is one-quarter of the pie. Your major competitor, unfortunately, has 50 percent of the market—half the pie. Six smaller manufacturers make up the rest of the market, and they each get a small sliver.

In an exploded pie chart one slice is pulled away for emphasis. If you wanted to use the above pie chart to highlight your share of the market, you could pull your 25-percent slice away from the rest of the pie.

9. Bar charts

A bar chart consists of a series of horizontal or vertical bars placed side by side. The relative length or height of each bar varies with the quantity the bar represents. Bar charts are used to show comparisons among quantities.

In an annual report, you might want to talk about how sales have increased over the last five years. To illustrate this point, you have a bar chart with five bars—one for each year's sales. If 1994 was your best year, that bar is longest. If sales in 1993 were only half those of 1994, the bar for 1993 would be half as long. This type of graph quickly allows the reader to see the changes that have been taking place from year to year.

10. Tables

A table is a body of data. It is used to handle a large amount of data too cumbersome to be covered in the body copy of the literature. Very short tables—those with one or two columns and only two or three items—can be run in the columns of text. Anything longer must be treated as a separate visual.

Tables don't have to be boring. You can, for example, print various sections of the table against different tints of color to add visual interest. Another technique is to separate each row of numbers or text with a slightly different band of color. Just be sure the colors and tints are light so that the text remains readable.

Drawings or Photos: How to Decide

The decision on whether to use artwork or photos is sometimes clear-cut and sometimes a tough call. Here are some guidelines to follow:

Use photographs if:

The product is sold on its visual appeal.   Some examples of products that appeal to consumers primarily because of how they look are designer clothing, sports cars, cosmetics, and jewelry.

The product is brand new.   In the case of a new restaurant, a personal computer, or new model car, prospective customers might need visual proof of the product's existence.

Your claims about the product require proof.   For example, if you claim that your chemical treatment makes swimming-pool water crystal-clear, your readers may be skeptical. You must prove your claim by showing before-and-after photographs of a pool treated with your compound.

You want to show product benefits.   Some benefits are a direct result of the product's design and appearance. For example, a photograph of the Apple IIC computer shows its portability. A photo of a Jeep shows the rugged construction. A photo of an open refrigerator shows the roomy interior. Use photographs in these cases, because showing a benefit is always better than just telling.

The product is attractive.   Perhaps your product is designed and packaged much more attractively than is your competitors. If this is the case, why not show off its superior visual appeal in an eye-catching photo?

If using a certain photo is optional, the decision on whether to use it may come down to whether the subject is attractive. Let's say you're producing a booklet on a charity foundation and are being pressured to include a photo of the foundation's acting president. If he's a friendly, kind-looking man, great! His picture will help bring in donations. If his appearance is passable, use the photo anyway. It will give him a much-deserved ego boost. But if he's an evil-looking codger who looks more like the head of a cult than a charity, you might consider leaving out the photo, or at least taking a new one that might make him look a bit more acceptable.

A series of photos can demonstrate the product.   Demonstration is a powerful sales technique for many products, especially those that the consumer is required to operate in some way (e.g., food processors, microwave ovens, squeeze-mops, venetian blinds, dishwashers). A series of photos, showing how to use the product step-by-step, can greatly increase the selling power of a brochure or flier.

Good photos already exist.   After you make a list of the photos you want to include in your new brochure, you may discover that some of these photos already exist in your files. That's a compelling reason for deciding in favor of photos. After all, the greatest reason to decide against photos is the cost. But if you already have the photo in hand, you eliminate the photographer's fee.

Photos would cost less.   If you're undecided as to whether to use a photo or drawing, and either would be equally appropriate, the cost may be the deciding factor. For a simple subject, an illustration may be less expensive, especially if you have to pay a photographer to travel to a distant shooting location. On the other hand, a complex color painting will probably cost more than a color photograph of the same subject.

Use illustrations if:

Art costs less than photography.   As I said, in some cases—those where art and photography are equally appropriate—hiring an artist may cost less than hiring a photographer. If you can save money without sacrificing effectiveness, use an illustration.

Artwork already exists.   Perhaps drawings created for previous promotions can be used as is or with minor modifications in your current project. If so, go ahead and use them. You'll save a lot of money by recycling artwork this way.

You need to illustrate a certain kind of concept. Location, function, construction, organization, quantity, proportions, and trends, are examples of concepts that are best represented by maps, diagrams, graphs, and charts.

You want to symbolize an idea or object. Symbols can be a convenient shorthand for communicating ideas and messages. Electrical engineers, for example, use simple symbols made of lines, squiggles, and circles to represent the various components used in circuits. A catalog of electronic components might use symbols at the top of each page to quickly identify the type of component listed on that page.

The product is unattractive. A good illustrator can create a realistic drawing that accurately depicts the product while masking (at least partially) its ugliness.

You need to prove the seriousness of your project. Many printed promotions try to sell people on projects and products that haven't been completed yet. A drawing can help convince the reader that the project is underway and fast becoming a reality.

Your visuals are designed to convey information. A schematic diagram or exploded view can say a lot more about the inner workings of an automobile engine or an attic fan than any photo can. Illustrations can have a much higher information content than photography. Use them to support text that explains complex systems, concepts, and technology.

You want to show the reader how to do something. Suppose you want to explain how to tile a floor, cut carpet, clean a fireplace, or install a screen window. It's hard to highlight the finer points of product construction or installation techniques with photographs. Illustrations are usually more effective for showing the reader how to install or use a product.

You want to create an atmosphere. Photographs are more limited in range of subject matter and style than drawings, because photos, after all, must reflect reality. An artist, on the other hand, can put on paper the wildest scenes the imagination can generate. When you want a piece of printed literature to evoke a powerful mood or atmosphere—somber and solemn, fun and frantic, solid and powerful—illustrations are the most effective tool you can use to create this environment.

The product can't be photographed.   It is impossible, for obvious reasons, to photograph an underground sprinkler once it has been installed. But an artist can easily create a rendering of the sprinkler as it is positioned under a lawn. The drawing can show how deep the sprinkler is laid, how it connects to the house plumbing, and how it delivers water to the lawn surface.

Doing Without Visuals

Properly used, visuals can greatly enhance the effectiveness of promotional literature. But an unnecessary visual—one that doesn't do anything to get your message across—creates clutter and weakens the piece.

Some brochure producers are under the impression that every brochure or flier must be illustrated. That just isn't true. There are many subjects that can't or shouldn't be illustrated, subjects that are more effectively promoted with an all-copy brochure.

How do you know when to omit visuals? Here are some tips to help guide you.

You should omit visuals if:

You're selling a service.   For many services, showing a picture of the service would be boring, meaningless, or both. Take accounting, for example. How would you illustrate a brochure promoting the services of a free-lance accountant? With a photo of the accountant punching buttons on his calculator or writing figures in his ledger? That's boring! Would you show a close-up of a completed income tax return? Also boring! You could possibly show some of the refund checks his clients have received from the IRS, but that is misleading and probably illegal.

If I were given the task of creating a brochure for this accountant, my initial plan would be to create an all-copy brochure. Later, as I worked on the project, I might discover a fresh, exciting way of visualizing the service and its benefits. But if I didn't, I would stick with an all-text treatment rather than force in a photo that didn't fit or, worse, was a boring, visual cliché.

The information doesn't need to be visualized.   Most non-fiction books, for example, contain no illustrations and do an excellent job of communicating information to the reader. If your topic naturally lends itself to illustration, then illustrate your pamphlet. But if the copy can get its message across without the aid of pictures, leave it alone. Don't clutter your pamphlet with extraneous drawings that serve as decoration but don't help you communicate with the reader.

You're selling an intangible.   Why, for example, does a person choose one doctor over another? Trust—in the doctor's ability and integrity. But trust is an intangible; you can't draw it or photograph it or put it in a picture. When selling intangibles, your *words* have to make the reader grasp the intangible and believe in it.

You're selling benefits, not features.   Perhaps you're selling, as the saying goes, "the sizzle, not the steak." In many cases, the reader is more interested in the benefits of the product—what it can do for her or him—than in what it is, how it works, or how it is put together.

Take accounting software as an example. Accounting software can turn your business from a sea of paperwork into a smooth-running, efficient, profitable operation. It can turn a jumble of numbers and ledgers and spread sheets into a lightning-fast information system that can put any figure or fact at your fingertips in seconds. This is one of the benefits of accounting software, and this is what makes it appeal to entrepreneurs and executives.

Your literature for such software could show sample screens of information or sample reports produced by the system. But these deal with the nitty-gritty and really don't reflect the benefits. Not only do they fail to support the main sales message; they may actually detract from it by painting a picture of those dreary rows of numbers the executive hopes to escape from. A marketer may decide to use an unillustrated brochure rather than include the typical software-literature photos showing screens and reports.

The suggested visuals are overused clichés.   Many visual subjects are so overused that they become clichés, visuals that had meaning once, but have been seen so often that they have lost all impact and effectiveness. These include the corporate executives sitting around the conference table, the smiling family enjoying the newest frozen food at the dinner table, the two housewives having an in-depth discussion on floor wax, and the happy secretary who is ecstatic about getting a new computer or workstation that will let her do even more work during the day.

Avoid these clichés. If the only visual you can come up with is the one everybody else has already used, consider dropping it and going to an all-copy brochure.

You don't have the budget.   If you don't have enough money to produce quality visuals, go to an all-copy treatment. You should use either use first-rate photos and artwork or no photos and artwork. It is better to omit visuals altogether than to ruin your literature by using messy, sloppy, or amateurish second-rate efforts.

The material on hand is of poor quality.   Perhaps you have photos and artwork available, but they stink. Don't use them. If you can afford to get new ones, do so. Otherwise, omit illustrations from your brochure.

Working With Illustrators

An illustrator is a person who draws or paints pictures. Unless you have hidden talent for drawing or have been studying at a local art school, you'll have to hire an illustrator to produce artwork for your literature. Here are some suggestions on how to get the best results for the most reasonable fee.

■ Know what you want
How many drawings do you want to commission? Are they simple or complex? Do you need color paintings or black-and-white line art? Rough sketches or realistic portraits?

Outline your requirements as specifically and completely as possible. Without a clear definition of your needs, you can't judge whether an artist is right for the job, and the artist can't give you an accurate cost estimate.

■ Choose the right artist for the job
First, ask for a résumé and client list. Has the artist studied at a good art school? Does he or she have a broad range of experience in handling commercial assignments? Who are the artist's clients? What kind of work was done for them?

Next, meet with the artist and take a look at the portfolio of sample work. There are three things to consider when evaluating a portfolio:

First impressions. Do you like what you see? You should be comfortable with the quality and appearance of the work the artist has produced to date.

Don't think that with the right coaching, a poor artist will perform miracles for you. Chances are, that won't happen.

Style. Does the artist's style mesh with your own? Is the style of illustration you see in the portfolio the style you want in your published brochure? Hire an artist who draws the way you want your artwork to look. Don't hire an artist who draws a different way and then try to force a change in style. It won't work.

Type of work. If you need architectural drawings, look for a portfolio containing good architectural drawings. If you need a diagram of a complex machine, hire an artist who has done extensive industrial and technical illustration. If you are putting out a brochure in comic book form, hire an artist who has free-lanced for Marvel or DC Comics. Choose an artist who has handled projects similar to yours.

■ Discuss fees in advance

Get a written cost estimate in advance and send the artist a purchase order before the work starts. Also, make sure you agree on how the job is to be charged. Do you pay for changes and revisions? Does the artist bill you after the job is completed or in stages? Do you pay on completion or on acceptance of the job? What constitutes an acceptable job, your subjective opinion or that of the artist or of an outside expert? These provisions should be settled now, in writing. Otherwise, they may have to be settled later, in court.

What will it cost? For small, simple line-art, black-and-white drawings, expect to pay anywhere from $150 to $250 per drawing. For full-size, more complex color renderings, the fee can be $300 to $500 or more each.

■ Provide complete background material

When you commission an artist to produce a drawing, provide as much background material and guidance as you can. If you want a rendering of a proposed corporate headquarters, provide all existing architect's drawings, blueprints, plans, and schematics. If you want a stylish version of a graph, have an engineer provide an accurate original the artist can work from.

Sit down with the artist and go over your preferences (if you have any) as far as style, color, size, and tone are concerned. Go to your clipping file and show samples of the look you are trying to achieve. You stand a better chance of getting what you want if you communicate your needs precisely, with both words and pictures.

■ **Explain your production requirements**

In order to produce a usable picture, the artist must be aware of how the drawing will be used and how it will be reproduced. Your best bet is to have the artist talk directly with the graphic designer or printer. This ensures that the artist produces an illustration that fits the layout and can be reproduced by the printing press.

■ **Build in review steps**

Have the artist submit the work in progress for your approval in several stages. Stage one could be a rough sketch, stage two the half-completed painting, stage three the finished work.

By reviewing the work in stages, you are assured that the job is proceeding according to your wishes. If you want to make changes, they can be done at a reasonable cost, much more reasonable than having the artist start over from scratch after completing the whole job.

How to judge the results

Has the artist done a satisfactory job? Usually, the answer is yes. Once in a while, though, you may be unsure of the results. How do you judge? First, compare the drawing to your expectations. If it looks like what you asked for, and is on the same level as the other work in the artist's portfolio, then you got what you paid for.

Another criterion is, "Will it do the job?" Maybe the drawing isn't as beautiful or as exciting as you thought it would be. Don't worry. Most artwork prepared for publication looks better in the finished brochure than it does as an original pasted to a piece of art board. Your main concern, though, is whether the artwork does what you want it to do—transmit information, show off a product's design, explain how something works, or explain how to use the product.

Have the same artist do all the artwork for a single piece of literature. An exception to this is literature with two or more types of illustrations that are drastically different, for example, a brochure that mixes color portraits with technical graphs. In such a case, the portrait artist might be unable to handle the graphs, and you'll have to put a second artist on the job.

Consistency is also a desirable virtue in a series of booklets or brochures. Try to use the same artist to illustrate the entire series; this gives it a family look.

Alternatives to Hiring an Artist

There are basically three alternatives to commissioning an original drawing from a professional artist:

■ Do it yourself

As I said earlier, unless you're a highly skilled amateur, forget it. A crude, unprofessional drawing can ruin an otherwise fine piece of literature. And even if you are good with watercolors or oil paints, you probably lack the graphic-arts know-how required to produce a picture suitable for a commercial job.

If you are good enough to do your own artwork, consult with your graphic designer first. Ask for an outline of any special requirements for the preparation of this artwork: size, proportions, color, and so on.

There are a number of computer programs designed to make it easier for nonartists to produce acceptable drawings. In desktop publishing jargon, these are called *paint programs*. Examples include Adobe Illustrator, Corel Draw, and Aldus Freehand.

With an optical scanner, you can scan into your computer system a piece of artwork, then use your paint program to modify the art to suit your needs. You can change the size, redraw portions, combine it with other artwork, or add colors.

■ Use clip art

Your local art supply store or dealer can sell you books of *clip art*: ready-to-use artwork you can clip and paste into your own layout. Most are black-and-white, but a few of the newer clip-art services now include color drawings in their books.

Today, many companies also offer clip art on computer disk or CD-ROM. Most of these disks contain computer-editable clip art, which means you can alter or redo the artwork using popular graphics and illustration programs.

The problem with clip art, of course, is that it is ready-made, hence, it covers subjects of a general nature and cannot be used to illustrate specific products, people, or organizations. A free-lance writer, looking to add a visual to his letterhead, might find a usable line drawing of a typewriter in a clip-art book. But if you need a more specific visual, such as a diagram of your product, you'll have to produce it yourself.

■ **Buy reproduction rights**

Occasionally, a trip to an art gallery or a glance at an art book may uncover a painting or drawing that would be perfect for your next brochure. If you can locate the artist or the artist's representative, you may be able to buy the right to reproduce the artwork in your literature. In such cases, you pay a fee and the artist supplies you with a color slide from which you can reproduce the work. The fee is based on the type of literature the art is to be used in and how many copies are printed. Your agreement with the artist may limit the number of years you can use the work.

11 Tips on Getting Good Photos

Most brochure producers use photographs as much or more than they use artwork. Here are 11 tips for getting the best photographs at reasonable cost.

1. Hire the right photographer for the job

Fees charged by free-lance photographers vary to an amazing degree. A top fashion or advertising photographer may command $2,000 or more for a single color shot. A moonlighter from your town paper, on the other hand, might be happy to put in a day's work and bill you only $300 for it. And why not? That day's fee may equal his regular weekly paycheck.

Of course, it's vitally important to hire the right photographer for the job. The newspaper photographer is the right choice for taking publicity photos, because he knows what appeals to editors. A family photographer may be best for shooting portraits of company officers, because she knows how to pose people to make their good features come through. A wedding photographer would be the one to capture the company banquet on film, because she has experience in handling groups at parties.

2. Plan a shoot list in advance

A *shoot list* is a list of the photographs that must be taken. Such a list helps you coordinate travel, sets, and props so the photographer can cover more ground in less time. If you can reduce the time it takes to shoot your photos from two days to one, you cut your photography fees in half.

Organize the list so that you complete all the shots in one area or location before you move on to the next. Schedule location shooting so you move to the nearest location each time, rather than hop back and forth. For each shot,

indicate what props, costumes, products, and models are required, so everything will be on hand when you arrive.

Even if you're only working on one or two brochures now, try to antici-
pate future photographic needs and get those photos taken *now*. The more
you get done in a single session, the more money you save. So if there's even
a possibility that you'll need a certain photo, take it. You can file it for later
use. And chances are that someone will request it sooner than you think.

3. Get permission

If you want to use a photograph of a person in your promotional literature, you
must get that person's permission in writing (See Figure 7.3). Otherwise, you
can be sued by that person for unauthorized use of her or his likeness. This
applies to professional models as well as to company employees, the photographer's friends and family, and people on the street.

Here's how attorney Richard Kurnit summed up the law in an article in
Advertising Age:

> The highest court in New York recently held that, even
> in cases in which there is no picture of a person's face, if
> the person can still be recognized his right of privacy has
> been violated. It also held that everyone involved—the
> photographer, the advertiser and even the medium car-
> rying the advertising—my be held liable.

Let's say you find an old photo that is perfect for your new brochure. If
the photo has people in it, and you can't track down the people to get their
signatures or find signed model release forms in your file, don't use it. You will
be leaving yourself open to a lawsuit.

Here is a model release form you can use to obtain permission to use a person's photograph in your literature. Make copies of this form or have your attorney create a form for you. Then get signatures from everyone appearing in your
photographs. I suggest you get signed release forms *before* the photo session
starts—not after. If a person appears in the day's batch of photos and then refuses to sign the form, you will have to scrap the photos and shoot them over again.

Figure 7.3 Sample model release form.

CONSENT OF SUBJECT OVER AGE _____

NAME _____

For a fee of $ _____ , which I have received,

I consent that the photographs taken on _____,
                                              (date)

or any reproduction of these photos, may be used by

_____ or by anyone to whom
            (name of organization)

give permission, for the purposes of illustration, advertising, promo-

tion, publicity, or publication in any manner. I also consent to the use

of my name in connection with these photographs.

NAME _____ DATE _____
              (signature)

ADDRESS _____

CITY _____ STATE _____ ZIP _____

WITNESS _____

4. Prepare the set

Preparing the set or location is the responsibility of the photographer, but you should be aware of what's involved so you can spot mistakes or suggest improvements when you supervise the photography session.

Preparing a set or location for shooting requires great attention to detail. The details are important, because even the smallest irregularity can ruin an otherwise fine photograph.

Here are some things to consider when supervising the preparation of a photo shoot:

Stick to classic styles. Everything in the scene should have a classic, timeless look. Objects that are fixed to the year or period can quickly date the photograph.

Wipe sweat.   Sweat on a lip or forehead can reflect the light from a photographer's flash bulb and cause a glare or hot spot in a photo. If your models perspire, wipe the moisture off and apply a little pancake powder to keep them dry.

Starch collars.   I once paid a professional to take a picture of me for the jacket of my first book. When I received the proofs, I was horrified; the left side of my collar was sticking out like a diving board. The photo appeared on the book and in many trade magazines, and to this day people ignore my good looks in the photo but continue to laugh at the stuck-out collar. So make sure collars are starched, ironed, and fixed in the proper position. Costumes and clothing with button-down collars are best, because these collars can't pop up.

Start early.   Shoot the photos with people early in the day when your subjects are fresh, their clothes unwrinkled, and the men's faces unmarked by five o'clock shadows. People look tired and worn by mid-afternoon, but products and other inanimate objects aren't bothered by time. Save the product shots for last.

Look for contrast.   Contrasting colors result in sharper-looking photos, whether you're shooting color or black-and-white. But if colors blend, the photos—especially the black-and-white shots—will come out dull and muddy. If you're shooting a male model in a sterile, white computer center, dress him in gray or black.

Maintain continuity.   If your brochure contains a series of related photographs, they should have continuity. That means that the background and the appearance of the models and props are the same from shot to shot. If you're using a series of photos to show how to operate a binding machine, the secretary shouldn't be wearing a pink blouse in one frame and a gray sweater in the next.

Keep it clean.   Clean up the set before you shoot. This means emptying the ash trays, picking up the trash, moving boxes out of the way, taking down bulletins and posters, repairing peeling paint, hiding broken furniture, cleaning up dirty machines. A single dirty item or piece of trash that seems insignificant may stick out in the actual photo.

Avoid lettering.   Amateur photographers often try to label items in their photos with placards and signs. *Don't.* This lettering won't be legible when the photo is reproduced in the brochure. If you have to label the photo, have an artist add the labels by hand to the print.

5. Make the photos appealing

A key reason for using photographs is to add visual appeal to the pages of a piece of printed literature. Therefore, it pays to make your photos as interesting to look at as possible.

One way to add interest is to use photos that tell a story. Most cologne ads, for example, show the bottle of cologne. But one recent ad showed a young man laying in his bed and talking on the phone. The bed was in an artist's loft, and unfinished canvasses dotted the room. The covers were half off, hinting that the man was nude. Who was this man? Whom was he talking to? What went on in that room last night? The photo began to tell a story which the copy went on to complete.

Even if you don't tell a story, you can heighten a photograph's appeal simply by adding people to it. If you're going to photograph a shirt, show someone wearing it. If you're taking a picture of a gourmet treat, show people eating and enjoying it.

Do not, however, photograph people or parts of their anatomy in extreme close-up. People are repelled by a face full of pores or the dirt under a thumbnail. Imperfections can be removed from photos using an air brush, but this is costly.

People like to know the size of a product, but you can't get a good grasp of size if you photograph the product alone against a plain background. Add a familiar object to the photo to give it a sense of scale. If you want to show the reader how compact a microchip is, for example, photograph it next to a penny or a postage stamp.

6. Frame the shot

Use your layout to guide the photographer in framing the shot. She'll frame it differently depending on whether you need a horizontal shot or a vertical shot.

Also, keep in mind what portion of the photo might be cropped (cut out) in production. Shoot so that you can crop the photo without cutting into its main subject matter; cropping should cut out extraneous background or borders only.

The newsletter *Communications Briefings* (volume 3, issue 9) reports that when cropping a photo, you should try for a height-to-width or width-to-height ratio of 3:2. This ratio is most pleasing to the human eye. Other pleasing ratios are 3:1, 5:3, and 8:5.

7. Decide on color or black and white

Let your photographer know whether you need color or black and white. Naturally, color slide film will be used for color and black-and-white film for black and white. If you need both, the photographer may bring two cameras and shoot both color and black and white, although good quality black-and-white prints can be made from color slides.

If you are taking pictures to be reproduced in full color, the photographer should use slide film and give you a slide or transparency. If you are taking pictures for black-and-white reproduction, the photographer should use any regular film and give you a black-and-white print.

Ask for prints with a matte (dull) finish instead of a silk (glossy) finish; matte prints reproduce better. Do not mount the print on a cardboard backing; many printing processes require that the print be flexible.

8. Don't be afraid to shoot too much

In deciding how many shots of a single setting or product to use, my philosophy is "the more, the better." If you've used multiple poses in a day's shooting, you have a greater variety to choose from when creating your mechanical.

Have the photographer take many different shots by trying different angles, using both posed and candid people shots, changing filters and lighting, using different lenses—anything to add variety and avoid the ho-hum of ordinary, bland, straight-on product photography.

9. Decide on a sales point

Each photo should add to the selling effectiveness of the brochure or catalog. If it doesn't, throw it out and use a different photo. Say you're producing a college catalog. The purpose is to get high school students to apply to the school. What photographs can be used to entice them? A shot of students catching a tan on the quad during a sunny day has its appeal. So does a photo of the science labs. A photograph of the school's power plant, on the other hand, may be a source of pride to the school's operating staff, but it won't bring in the applications. Make sure every photo you use has sales appeal.

10. Avoid clichés

As with illustrations, avoid clichés when planning and taking photographs. "There's always that person with a piece of paper who has to be photographed," laments photojournalist Arthur Rothstein, "a student with a diploma, a president of a corporation giving a check to someone. You've got to avoid cliché shots of these repetitive, routine situations by looking at them in a fresh, imaginative way." One way of doing this, says Rothstein, is with a candid shot.

11. Consider using special effects

The appearance of photographs can be altered using a variety of special effects. Two of the most popular are *airbrushing* and *screening*.

An airbrush is a paint atomizer powered by an electric motor. It produces a fine spray of paint that the airbrush artist, also known as a *retoucher*, applies to a color print. Airbrushing can be used to alter the photograph so that it shows things that weren't there or hides things that are. For example, let's say you photograph a glass full of whiskey and then decide that the glass should have been half empty. You send the print to the retoucher, and when it comes back, the glass is half empty. You cannot tell that the print has been retouched.

If you examine newspaper photographs with a magnifying glass, you can see that they consist of a series of closely spaced dots. The dots allow the photo to have shades of gray as well as black and white. Any picture in which the shading is achieved through the use of dots is called a *halftone*.

Halftones are made by converting regular photo prints with a *dot screen*. But by using a *line screen* instead of a dot screen, an ordinary photo can be turned into a special effect. To begin with, the line screen eliminates shades of gray, leaving only a stark image of black and white. By using different screens, different patterns in the photo can be created: straight lines, wavy lines, spirals. You can even order a customized screen that can be used to etch a special pattern into photos—your corporate logo, for example.

Line screens are an especially effective technique for breathing life into dull or poor-quality prints. A picture that seems flat and boring as a regular halftone may make an intriguing graphic when it is processed with a line screen.

Stock Photos

Besides hiring a free-lance photographer, there are other places you can turn to when you need photographs.

A *stock house* is a firm that maintains a large library of photos covering almost every subject imaginable. When you need a particular subject—a clown, a group of children, a blue sky with clouds, the beach at dawn—get in touch with a local stock house. It'll send you a catalog or else a number of representative shots to choose from. If you see something you like, you tell the stock house how you plan to use it (type of publication, number of copies) and it'll quote you a fee. This can range from $100 to over $1,000, depending on the application. In some cases it may be cheaper to hire a photographer to take the shot from scratch. One of the largest stock photo houses is The Image Bank in New York City, (212) 529-3080.

Stock houses are not the only source of stock photography. Government agencies, newspapers, wire services, nonprofit organizations, museums, and corporate public relations departments all have photo files that may be available to you. NASA, for example, sells striking color photography of space shots and moon missions at a very reasonable cost. Manufacturers often provide free photographs to their dealers and distributors for use in local advertising and promotion. A magazine or newspaper that does a story about your firm may be willing to let you use the photos from their article in your own sales literature and promotional publications.

CHAPTER EIGHT

SPECIAL MARKETING PROBLEMS (AND HOW TO SOLVE THEM)

This chapter discusses common problems encountered when planning and producing brochures, and suggests ways of handling them effectively.

The Product Keeps Changing

This is a major headache for high-tech and service companies. Their products and services are in a constant state of evolution, so any published material quickly goes out of date.

One solution is to wait until the product becomes relatively stable in design and function before publishing any literature on it. But that's a mistake. Without literature, your advertising and promotion campaign is crippled. The fact is that many consumers—and almost all business buyers—won't make a purchase without first receiving some type of printed material. Without a product brochure, you lose these sales.

A better alternative is to publish a temporary brochure as an interim solution. The company can get by with this small, inexpensively produced piece until it feels secure in spending the money for a real brochure.

The interim piece can be produced inexpensively in-house using a desktop publishing system, with the brochures printed in small quantities. This prevents obsolescence and eliminates being stuck with a stack of costly color brochures that are out of date and unusable.

If, for example, you envision a major product update in six to eight months, don't print more than a six-month supply. Normally, I recommend that you print more copies than you think you'll need, because of the small incremental cost addition as opposed to a short run. But if your brochure will be outdated soon, order fewer copies so there will be less waste.

If your brochure must be updated frequently or be customized to specific markets or even specific customers, and your print runs are very short (under 200 copies), you might want to store the copy and design in electronic format on disk, then print out the brochures one at a time on your laser printer.

Several companies offer special papers and ready-made brochure templates. These templates are sheets of good-quality paper that are cut and folded in brochure format; you run the template blank through your laser printer, printing your text, then refold the template to make a finished brochure.

The largest nationwide supplier of such brochure templates is Paper Direct in Lyndhurst, New Jersey. For a free catalog of their templates and special papers for laser printers, you can call toll-free 800-A-PAPERS.

When you plan the brochure, create a layout that leaves room for changes and revisions. Leave extra white space on the page so you can add to the copy without redoing the page layout. Leave room to expand tables, charts, and lists that will grow in size as your product line expands. If the basic design of the product is set and only certain technical specifications will change, put these specifications in a separate table so you can update them without resetting the type for the entire text of the piece. Plan for change so the copy and layout can be updated without having to redesign the brochure from scratch.

The Product Doesn't Exist Yet

Yes, I've been asked many times to write copy for a product that hasn't been built or produced yet, or for a service that is still only in the conceptual stage.

Because of the long lead-time required to produce and implement an advertising campaign, many manufacturers start producing literature, ads, and other materials before the product is actually built. When a major manufacturer produced a brochure describing a new electronic filing system, the only such system in existence was the crude experimental model set up in the manufacturer's test lab. The exterior design of the equipment hadn't even been decided on.

The art studio will have difficulty creating a layout for a nonexistent project. Why? Because they have to show the customer what the product looks like without letting on that it hasn't actually been built yet.

The artist has several ways of doing this.

One way is to use photographs of a *prototype*, a full-size, functioning, experimental version of the product. If the actual manufactured product will be a carbon copy of the prototype, you can use photos of the prototype to illustrate your brochure. Readers have no way of knowing that the machine they are looking at was the only one of its kind at the time. If the actual product will be different in appearance from the prototype, photos of the prototype should not be used. The product the readers see in the literature should look exactly like the one they buy.

The next best thing to a prototype is a *mock-up*. The mock-up is a model of the product; it looks exactly like the product, but is a fake, with no parts, wires, or gears inside. Use mock-up photos only if the mock-up looks 100 percent authentic, a phony-looking mock-up photo is easy to spot.

But whether you show a prototype or mock-up, try to include some sort of product photograph in any literature for a new product. Photos convince customers that the product is real, whereas new-product literature with only drawings gives the impression that the product doesn't really exist.

In some cases, you may not be able to photograph a prototype, model, or product sample, and you will have to use artwork to depict the new product. Your illustrations should be as realistic as possible to create the illusion that the product is real. Use blueprints, engineering drawings, exploded diagrams, or a high-quality color illustration. Avoid rough sketches, line drawings, and abstract or "stylized" artwork that can give the literature a phony look.

The Product Is Sold to Multiple Markets

Recently a company needed to produce a brochure on its new moisture analyzer, a machine that detects even the slightest bit of moisture in air, gas, liquids, or solids. But the problem was that the device was used in many different industries and for different applications: utilities, rubber plants, chemical plants, food processing, textiles, natural gas pipelines, tobacco curing. And each of these buyers bought moisture analyzers for different reasons.

If your product appeals to a variety of different prospects, and each group is motivated by different product benefits, you must ask the question: "Can a single brochure be effective in selling to all markets? Or do I need a separate piece of literature for each group of buyers?"

It depends. If, as in the case of the moisture analyzer, the product offers unique benefits to each market, you may want to create a series of folders, each highlighting how the product meets the needs of a particular group of buyers.

On the other hand, some products—light bulbs, for example—are bought for the same reasons regardless of the market (schools, industry, offices, consumers). So there's no need to create market-specific literature for a light bulb.

In some cases, the basic reason for buying the product is the same for all buyers, but you may want to highlight specific applications in each area. If that's the case, there's no need for separate brochures; instead, you can devote a page of your brochure to listing these applications by market.

Some products might be sold to different markets, but each market likes to believe the product is designed especially for it. The brokerage firm buys a business phone system for the same reason a manufacturer does: to communicate. But brokers think they are special, as most of us do. They want to buy a phone system specifically designed for brokerage houses.

Don't rush out and create a special brochure for this market just yet. There's a better way: You can create the impression that a brochure is aimed at specific markets by printing one basic brochure with different covers. For example, a different cover photo could be used with each version. The brokerage-house brochure shows a stockbroker in an office, surrounded by ticker tape and talking on the phone system. A different version, aimed at plant engineers, shows a hard-hat shop steward talking on the shop floor.

You can add to this differentiation with other techniques. The color of the cover, for example, might be different for each version—green for brokerage houses, blue for manufacturers, yellow for utilities. You could also print a line of copy on each cover to identify the specific market (e.g., "The communications tool for brokerage firms" or "The system that lets manufacturers communicate").

The Product Is Sold to Multiple Buying Influences

Packaged goods—soap, shampoo, cereal, soda—are bought by one person: the consumer who uses them or buys them for the family. With other consumer products, you have to appeal to more than one customer. Toy advertisements, for example, must make the children want the toy as well as convince the parents that the toy is safe, educational, wholesome, and worthwhile.

When you sell products and services to business, the situation becomes even mere complex. Business purchases are usually made by committee, not by individuals. For example, if you are selling a $500,000 pollution-control system to a chemical plant, many people are involved in the purchase: the plant manager, the purchasing agent, the president of the firm, the pollution-control expert, and possibly others. The problem is that each of these people has a different level of interest in and understanding of your product. The purchasing agent is primarily concerned with cost. The plant manager is worried about installation and maintenance. The pollution-control expert will analyze whether your product can handle the requirements of removing chemicals and particulates from the air. And top management is more concerned with the reputation and reliability of your firm.

If you want to influence a wide range of buyers, you have to take this into consideration in the planning of your literature. Some advertisers find it advantageous to create two or more levels of literature. The first brochure is more sales-oriented and is aimed at managers, purchasing agents, and others who want compelling reasons to buy your product but don't have the time or patience for the nitty-gritty. The second brochure is more detailed. It is aimed at operators, technicians, engineers, and other experts who hunger for complete knowledge. It gives them the numbers, figures, graphs, and curves that would not be of interest to less technically oriented buyers.

A more economical approach is to create a single piece of literature that is interesting and appealing to a broad audience. This takes some extra planning in the design and copywriting stages. The copy style, for example, must be readable enough to catch the interest of a busy manager, but it must not be so general or full of fluff that it turns off the technical reader. Highly technical material should be collected and displayed in a separate section of the brochure (such as the centerfold or sidebar) so that technical readers can easily find it and executives can skip over it.

Creating a lot of different pieces of literature is expensive, so I recommend that you try to produce a single brochure that tells the whole story and appeals to all audiences. If your audience is so diverse that this approach is too cumbersome, then additional pieces of literature may be required. But before you commit yourself to a second or a third or a fourth piece of literature, ask yourself, "Is this really necessary? Or is there some way to say it all in my central brochure?" Cutting down on the number of pieces of literature you publish saves time and money. It also eliminates confusion and error when fulfilling inquiries.

The Sales Cycle Has Multiple Steps

The number of steps in the sales cycle is determined by counting how many times there is contact—in person or via promotion—between seller and buyer. In direct-mail fundraising, for example, the fund-raiser sends a letter to you requesting a donation. If you believe in the cause and are moved by the letter, you send your donation by mailing a check or a pledge card. The sale is made in one step.

But let's say you are in the market for a new car. There may be many steps between your initial interest and the final purchase. The first step is watching a car commercial on TV. The second step is visiting the dealer's showroom. The third step is studying the manufacturer's brochure on the car and thinking about it at home. The fourth step is going back to the showroom, negotiating a deal, and writing a check for the down payment.

Generally, the number of steps involved increases with the cost of the product. And often, the advertiser is unsure as to whether to try for a quick sale by combining or skipping steps, or to put less pressure on the buyer by adding some steps to the sales cycle.

You must consider your sales cycle when you plan your promotional literature. If the cycle has multiple steps, can one piece of literature be used to satisfy all requirements? Or will you need a separate piece of literature for every step: one brochure to respond to inquiries, a second to offer more detailed information, a third to be used by salespeople during sales calls, a fourth to close the sale?

The answer, naturally, depends on your particular product, customer, and selling methods. Only you, after a careful analysis of your situation, will know how many, and what type, of brochures you need.

When possible, make one piece do double or triple duty in your sales cycle. For example, many companies use a very brief, general brochure to respond to inquiries and a more comprehensive brochure for sales calls. But there's really no reason to make the inquiry piece so general; after all, the person requesting it has demonstrated an interest in your product. By adding more meat to the inquiry piece, you can create a brochure that can work in both environments.

Product Features Change Periodically

This is the case with automobiles, among other products. The 1994 Honda Accord is, after all, just a variation of the 1993 model. Yet the differences are significant enough that Honda annually produces new brochures to describe this year's models.

Of course, you are not Honda, and producing a brand new four-color brochure every 12 months may be a strain on your budget. What can you do? The first thing is to ask yourself whether you really need a new brochure in the first place. Perhaps the change is so insignificant that it doesn't need to be described in your literature. Or maybe it can be handled with some type of separate insert sheet or envelope stuffer. If not, you can still save money by recycling your old brochure rather than scrapping it and starting from scratch. Some product changes, for example, are purely cosmetic: a new package, a new label, a new case or housing. What's inside remains the same. So you can keep your copy and layout. Just photograph the new product and substitute these new photos for the outdated ones in the brochure.

Yes, you'll have to change the printing plates, and printing a new batch of bulletins is costly. But it's not nearly as costly as setting new type, doing new page layouts, or writing entirely new copy.

Other changes, while substantial, do not change the essence of the product or your sales pitch. Making these changes can be as simple as changing the numbers in a table of product specifications or adding a couple of paragraphs of copy to the brochure. Again, you pay for redoing the printing plates and printing new bulletins, but it costs less than a complete rewrite and redesign.

Unfortunately, some changes completely alter the nature of the product and your sales pitch. In these cases, there's no choice but to redo the brochure. But you can still save money by recycling as much of the old brochure as possible: cover design, photos, tables, charts, illustrations, even sections of type.

If your brochure needs to be redone frequently, have it produced on a desktop publishing system using page-layout software so that the entire document—text, layout, graphics, and visuals—can be stored on disk as an electronic file. This makes it faster, easier, and less expensive to create revisions: You just make your changes on the disk, take it to a service bureau to produce a new film, and take it to your printer.

The Company's Various Products Seem Unrelated

At first glance, this doesn't seem to be a problem at all. Just create a separate brochure for each product and distribute the brochures to the appropriate buyers. But a random offering of products and services creates confusion among your customers. Consumers tend to form an image of a company in their minds: Apple is a computer company, Ford a car company, and Gerber's a baby-food company. But what if Ford suddenly started marketing a personal computer? Mass confusion! People would say, "Hey, wait a minute. What does this have to do with cars and trucks?" And they would stick with the traditional makers of computers: IBM, Apple, Dell, Compaq.

And so it is with your organization. People know you by your products, services, or goals. If you add new products or services that don't fit in with your current line, people will become confused. To overcome this confusion, try to find a common element that can link seemingly disparate products, a unifying theme that provides a consistent identify.

For instance, a mail-order firm in New York state sells *planning boards* (oversized wall calendars you can use to organize and schedule the work flow in your department or organization). Recently, the company began offering books by mail. When it added books to its catalog, that created confusion. Why is a manufacturer of planning boards in the publishing business?

Then the marketing people at the firm realized that the common element of the books and the boards was that both products help companies improve productivity through better organization, planning, and thinking. (Their books deal solely with business topics, such as management, marketing, and communications.) They created a new theme for their catalog, one based around the slogan, "Planning tools to help you increase productivity." The theme made sense out of the combination of books and boards and eliminated confusion among the customers.

When you add a product or service, study it to see if you can discover a relationship between the new item and your current line. If you can't—if there is absolutely no tie-in—perhaps the product is wrong for your line.

Components Are Packaged or Sold Individually

In a corporate brochure for a major bank, the challenge was to describe the overall capabilities and business philosophy of the bank as well as to outline the various services it offers to its customers. Some customers buy a package consisting of every service. But many others are interested in only one or two services.

To make matters even more complex, the bank has a special accounting system through which every service is handled. This is a major advantage of using the bank, because the system generates extra interest for customers using the service. In addition to this benefit, which is common to all services, each service has its own unique advantages over the competition.

How did the bank handle this? It created a central brochure that described the bank, its philosophy, and its unique accounting method and how that method makes using the bank's services more profitable. The information in this central brochure stressed the bank's superiority as an organization and mentioned the individual services only in general terms. The last page of the brochure contained a pocket. Into this pocket were inserted seven fliers, each describing in detail a specific service of the bank. The fliers also briefly mentioned the advantage of the special accounting system. But they didn't explain it in depth, because the central brochure took care of that.

The bank's sales representatives could then use the individual fliers to sell specific services to select customers. The customer interested in service G could get all the information she needed in a brief flier, without having to plow through a huge brochure on services A, B, C, D, E, and F first.

In addition, the bank adds and changes services from time to time. Now, when a service is added, it simply updates and reprints one of the inexpensive fliers rather than the expensive corporate brochure.

The Brochure Can't Adequately Sell the Product

Print does have its limits. Try, for example, to write a paragraph describing the scent of a rose or the taste of lobster, and you'll immediately see these limitations at work.

Don't be frustrated by this. Instead, try to understand what printed promotional literature can do—and what it cannot do.

Let's say a TV manufacturer asks you to produce a brochure describing its new color TV. Your brochure can show pictures of the set and the screen. But what it can't do is demonstrate the product; a printed photo is a poor substitute for seeing the set in operation. This may frustrate you until you stop to consider that no one is going to order an expensive color TV sight unseen, anyway. People will go to the store and watch the TV; the brochure is just something they can take home and study at their leisure before making a purchasing decision.

By the way, advertisers are becoming more and more ingenious in overcoming the limitations of printed literature. Some cosmetics companies, for example, include scratch-and-sniff cards with their literature; when you scratch the card, you smell the fragrance. Many mail-order record companies, realizing that you won't want to buy a record until you've heard part of it, bind in small, plastic demonstration records in their mailings. The prospect plays the demonstration record and, if she likes it, she sends for the full-length record or record set.

The Product or Service Can't Be Illustrated

How do you illustrate financial planning, free-lance writing, life insurance, career counseling, legal counsel, a seminar, or the preparation of income tax forms? There are many products and services that don't easily lend themselves to illustration. And there are two ways to overcome the problem.

The first is to hire a designer clever enough to come up with visual concepts for these hard-to-illustrate products. Even if you are unable to make any suggestions, don't worry. Just hand over all the background information and let the designer go to work. When the initial ideas are presented as thumbnail sketches, you can judge whether the artist has hit the target or missed the mark.

The second solution is simply to omit visuals and have an all-text brochure. There are many successful brochures that consist solely of words.

The Product Is Ugly

You may be faced with the tough task of selling a product that is not designed and packaged as attractively as it could be: a book with an ugly cover; a computer with a plain, box-like terminal; a cosmetics set in an unattractive wrapper.

What can you do? Here are some options:

Don't show the product.   A book, for example, is bought more for its contents than for its cover. If you're writing a promotion to sell a poorly designed book by mail, don't show a picture of the cover in your flier. Although an unattractive cover may prevent people from buying a book, once they do make a purchase based on the book's contents and merits, they are highly unlikely to return it just because the cover isn't fancy. So, if your product is ugly, don't show it.

Use a sketch.   A sketch, carefully executed, can accurately portray the product while making it appear less gruesome than it really is.

Redesign the product or the package.   If the merchandise is really that hard to look at, maybe you should redesign the product or the package before you put it on the market.

Lawyers Tie Your Hands and Rewrite Your Copy

Here's how it happens: After months of planning, writing, and approvals, an organization has a manuscript and layout they are happy with. Before it is published, someone suggests they "run it by legal."

The brochure copy is sent to the lawyers. One week, then two, then three go by. The advertising manager begins to worry. Then, one morning, she gets the manuscript back on her desk. Attached is a memo informing her that legal approves the copy "as per the revisions indicated on the manuscript."

And some revisions! What started out as a lively, powerful, persuasive piece is now a dull, turgid, dead document—copywritten by lawyers instead of writers. The lawyers have taken out all the specifics and all direct claims, watering the prose down with generalities and hedge words. The result is something so stiff and lifeless that no prospect or customer would dream of struggling through the copy. It is a document that pleases legal but no one else.

Don't let this happen. If you feel that it's necessary to have your legal department or outside counsel review your copy, then have them do it. But don't let the lawyers rewrite copy. Instead, have them outline the specific factual changes they recommend. Go over each revision to make sure the change is necessary from a legal standpoint and not just the personal whim of the attorney. Then, have the copy revised by a writer or an editor. Writing should be repaired by writers. Don't let your lawyers moonlight as copywriters.

You Can't Give Away Too Many Trade Secrets

Many organizations are afraid of being too specific in their literature because they don't want the competition to learn their trade secrets. But if your literature lacks facts and specifics, it becomes weak and ineffectual.

What can you do? My advice is to write the best, most fact-filled literature you can and not worry about the competition. Why? Because if your competitors want to learn more about your product, they will. (For example, they can, under a false identity, buy your product, go to your dealership, or even pump your salespeople for information over the phone.) So there's no point in crippling your promotional literature by holding back the facts that can help the literature do its job of selling the product.

Don't, of course, publish trade secrets that are secret even to your customers. But you should publish a piece of information if it helps you make the sale. Remember, if it's something you'd say to a customer in confidence, it's something your competitors can learn if they really want to. So quit worrying about spilling the beans and concentrate on creating great promotional literature.

The Product Is New and Unproven

True, new means exciting and able to attract new prospects. But it also indicates a product that is untested and unproven, one that has not demonstrated its ability to perform as advertised.

In the same way, many people are afraid to buy from new companies. They reason, "This new company is a small fledgling enterprise competing among established giants. Its future is uncertain. If I buy the product and the company goes out of business in a year, I will be stuck with a product that no one will service or support."

You can see the problem that a new product poses to the brochure writer. Should you stress its newness, thereby generating excitement and interest but raising questions as to the product's reliability and performance? Or should you skirt the issue of newness, thereby eliminating the questions but also the opportunity to generate excitement?

My answer is this: Go all out in stressing the newness in your brochure. Splash the cover with words like *Introducing*, *Announcing*, and *Now Available*. Make a big to-do about the product being new and different. It will make your brochure, and your product, stand out from the crowd.

Then, in your copy, you must take pains to offset the questions of reliability and proven performance that the aura of newness raises. Here are some ways to do it:

- Mention that although the product is new in the United States, it has proven its performance for five years in Europe and other countries overseas.

- If the product is an industrial product adapted for consumer use, say so. Let's say you're selling a scaled-down version of an industrial paint-sprayer designed for home use. Explain that although the new version is being offered to the consumer market for the first time, it is based on a machine that has gained great favor among professional painters over a period of many years.

- Many products are first test-marketed on a small, local scale before being offered nationwide. If this is the case with your product, say so. Explain that hundreds of buyers in Kansas or Ohio or Florida have been delighted with the product and so you are making it available to people in all 50 states.

- Some products have been around for years but have never really been promoted. If yours is such a product, you can announce it as new. Then explain that although it is new in the sense of being marketed nationwide for the first time, it has delighted a limited but loyal group of customers for many years.

- Maybe your product really *is* brand new. Maybe it hasn't been sold to a single consumer. But it has been thoroughly tested in your laboratory and in the field. Highlight these test results in your copy to show that the product has proven its performance under rigorous conditions.

The Product Is Going to Change Soon

And you know what these changes are. Should your literature describe the product as it is today or as it will be when the changes are made?

This is a tough one. Here are some guidelines to follow in such a situation:

Avoid using future-tense references. People become uncomfortable if they keep reading about features that "will be available" or are "soon to come." They expect a brochure to tell them about a product as it really is now, not as the manufacturer dreams it will be. So your brochure should reflect reality.

Make an occasional promise. It's okay to talk about one or two forthcoming improvements or features, as long as you don't overdo it. The reader can accept a few promises if they are isolated and if the copy makes clear that they are planned improvements and not existing features. Just make sure that 95 percent or more of your copy is grounded in the present.

Don't dream out loud. Talk about only those planned improvements that are on the drawing board and fast on their way to becoming reality. Give the reader a preview of next year's model, if you wish. But don't make your brochure a wish-list of all the conceivable features you'd like to add but may never get around to designing. People have a long memory when it comes to broken promises.

Don't discuss planned changes in the present tense. Some advertisers say, "Write about planned features and upcoming products as if they already exist. After all, by the time the brochure is published, they will be available for sale."

If you use this tactic, be absolutely certain that the product change will be made according to schedule. It anything goes wrong, and the change discussed in the literature isn't made in the product, you will be stuck with a pile of brochures that contain misinformation.

CHAPTER NINE

PRODUCTION TIME!

Now the job is more than halfway done. After just a few final steps—typesetting, mechanicals, film, and printing—you'll have the finished literature in your hands.

Your role here is primarily that of supervisor and checker. You must carefully supervise the work of your outside vendors to make sure the job is being done properly and according to your specifications. And you must check the work every step of the way to ensure that the brochure will be accurate and error-free. There will be a lot of proofreading to do at this stage!

Here, briefly, is what's going to happen next:

Your graphic artist will have the text of your brochure set in type. He will buy the type from a place known as a *type house*, *typesetter*, *typographer*, or *compositor*. Or, more likely, he will take a disk containing your text to a *service bureau* and have type generated directly from diskette using a high-resolution image setter or laser printer. You can, if you wish, deal with the type house or service bureau directly, but if you have hired a graphic artist, it's better to have it done for you.

The type—body copy and headlines—will be pasted up on pieces of stiff cardboard known as *art board*. The size and location of all visuals will also be indicated on this board. Such a paste-up of copy and art is known as a *mechanical* or *board*. If your brochure was created using desktop publishing software, you may not need to create a mechanical. Instead, a high-resolution image setter can convert your computer files directly to film negatives from which the printer can reproduce your brochures.

The printer will take the mechanical or film and reproduce your literature on the paper you have selected. If your literature includes full-color photography, the printer will have to send the job out to a *color separator* in order to reproduce these pictures.

You pay the printer and receive your literature. Everybody lives happily ever after.

Let's take a look at how you can control quality and cut costs at each step of the way.

Typography

Phototypesetting

Typography (called *type* for short) is lettering printed as black characters on a glossy photographic film or laser printer paper.

The type can be cut apart with a razor and pasted on art board manually; in years past, it was always done this way. Now graphic artists, using desktop publishing systems and page layout software, can do page layout directly on the computer screen.

Once the layout looks good on the screen, the designer can print a proof directly on a laser printer or have a service bureau produce a camera-ready mechanical on an image setter.

In the past, to get your brochure set in type (a process known as *typesetting*), you had to take the manuscript to the typesetter (or have your artist do it for you). The typesetter would manually retype your manuscript onto a computer keyboard. The keyboard activated a special phototypepsetting machine that produced a copy of your text set in type. The type came out in one long sheet. The typesetter would send over a *galley* (proof copy) of this sheet for your approval.

Because the typesetter could make mistakes when retyping your manuscript, you had to carefully proofread the galley to catch any errors. (See the section on proofreading later in this chapter.) The galley would then be returned to the typesetter, corrections would be made, and your artist would get clean, error-free type to work from.

Type houses still exist and a number of graphic design companies—usually those producing full-color brochures, annual reports, and other high-level printed promotional pieces—still work this way. But more and more brochure producers these days are using *electronic typesetting* rather than the manual or phototypesetting process just described.

Electronic typesetting

Here's how electronic typesetting works:

You start with text in electronic form. If you or your copywriter wrote your brochure copy using a computer, then you can provide copy on disk to the graphic artist.

If you have the text typed but not on disk, you can have it scanned and converted to disk. A service bureau or desktop publishing service equipped with an optical scanner can scan your manuscript and convert it to disk format. They must have a clean original typed copy to scan; a photocopy or fax is not acceptable. One company that converts documents to disk via optical scanning is Doc-U-Scan in Whippany, New Jersey, phone (201) 993-9363.

Although some service bureaus and desktop designers can work with different disk formats and convert your disk to their format, it's a plus if you can provide copy on a disk in a format with which they are compatible.

Start with disk size. Most graphic designers work on the Macintosh and therefore use 3½″ diskettes. If you use 5¼″ diskettes, ask your artist whether these can be converted in-house or through a service bureau. If you are upgrading your computer or getting a new one, I recommend you have two floppy disk drives, one of each size. This will ensure you can provide the proper size disk for any outside vendors you use.

If you use the same word-processing software as your art studio, your disk will be completely compatible with theirs. Among corporate PC users, WordPerfect seems to be the number-one choice of word-processing software.

Some word-processing programs have as a built-in feature the ability to convert files to other word-processing formats. If yours does not, then ask your designer if she wants the diskette in WordPerfect (or WordStar, or whatever it is you or your copywriter write in) or ASCII format.

ASCII (short for American Standard Code for Information Interchange) is a standard code that allows computers to convert characters, numbers, and symbols into the numerical binary code that the machine can understand. Almost all designers using PCs can work with a disk in ASCII format if you cannot provide copy in the particular format they use. Or, you can use an outside disk-conversion service to convert your diskettes to the format desired by your graphic designer or desktop publishing service. One such service is NDC in New York City, phone (212) 463-7511.

The graphic artist takes your diskette, then electronically converts your text into type using word-processing software, font packages, and page layout programs. A *font package* is computer software that electronically "sets" regular text in various fonts or type styles. The page layout program arranges this type in the desired layout on the screen.

Once the type is set electronically in the correct size and type style and laid out in proper position on the screen, the graphic artist can output this file to a laser printer, for making a proof for review, or to a higher resolution image setter that generates camera-ready layout.

Electronic typesetting eliminates the time-consuming, error-prone task of rekeying the copywriter's manuscript into the computer or typesetting device by hand. This reduces mistakes, saves time, and lowers cost.

How to specify type

The term *specify type* means to select type in the size, style, and format you want. This should be done by the artist because there are so many variables involved. However, you should be aware of the basic considerations involved in specifying type, as described below.

Size. Size refers to the height of the lettering. It is measured in *points*, and there are 72 points to an inch. Most newspapers are set in 8- or 9-point type; most promotional literature in 10- to 12-point. Another commonly used measure is the *pica*; 1 pica is equal to 6 points. Some artists also measure in *agates*; there are 14 agates to the inch.

Style. There are hundreds of "families" (basic styles) to choose from. The two basic categories of type styles are *serif* and *sans serif*. Serif type has little lines and curls on the ends of the letters; sans serif doesn't. This book is set in a serif type, and serif is generally believed to be more readable than sans serif. Serif is usually used for body copy; headlines and subheads are often in sans serif.

Typeface. You also need to specify the typeface within the family with respect to thickness of the lettering (light, medium, or bold), width of the characters (some families offer a variety of condensed or extended faces), and slant or *posture* (the angle of the type).

Case. This term refers to whether the letters are capitalized (upper case) or not (lower case). Setting type in all caps makes it difficult to read and, if done for emphasis, should be used sparingly.

Kerning.   This refers to the spacing between the letters in a word. Too much space makes the type look thin and airy; too little makes it appear scrunched.

Spacing between words.   You can choose regular spacing or narrower (*French*) spacing.

Leading.   This refers to the space between each line of type. Unlike typewriters, which offer only single, double, and triple spacing, typesetting machines and desktop publishing system can adjust spacing from 1 point to as many as you choose. Most graphic artists space lines of type 1 or 2 points apart.

Justification.   The type is justified when the completed line is filled and both right and left margins are *flush* (even). If it is not justified, one or both margins (commonly only the right) are *ragged* (uneven). Both the left and right margins of this book are flush, so the book is set with justified type.

Column width.   Column width is measured in inches, picas, or characters (number of letters and spaces). In a brochure with full-size (8½″ × 11″) pages, the columns are about 2¼ inches wide if the type is set in three columns, and 3½ inches wide if type is set in two columns. When setting columns, three and a half inches is about the widest a column should be; if it is any wider, the text becomes difficult to read.

Indentations.   Also to be decided is the number of spaces (called *em* spaces) by which lines (such as the first line of a new paragraph) should be indented.

Paragraph spacing.   Some designers prefer to leave an extra space between paragraphs to make the copy a bit easier to read.

Proofreading

You will have an opportunity to proofread your brochure copy at several different stages:

- Final, revised copy manuscript submitted by copywriter

- Proof or *live comp* of rough layout submitted by graphic designer
- Proof of mechanical to be submitted to the printer
- Final proof (printer's bluelines)

At each step, proofread the type carefully. Because the brochure production process is mostly electronic from start to finish these days, making changes is easier and far less time-consuming and costly than it used to be in the days when everything was done by hand.

As a rule, however, changes cost less when you spot them earlier, more when you spot them as the brochure nears its final form. Therefore, be especially diligent when proofing early versions; don't adopt the attitude that you can catch all the mistakes later; it will slow you down at the later stage and cost you more.

When proofreading, go through the copy and *neatly* mark all changes and corrections. Use the standard proofreader's marks found in any good dictionary, or your own notation, as long as corrections are legibly marked and easily understood by others. You should also proofread the page proofs against the original manuscript to make sure nothing has been changed or left out.

If the typesetter or design studio has made a typographical error, there is no charge for the correction. But if you decide to change the copy at this point, this is known as an *author's alteration* (or *AA*), and you must pay for it. That's why the copy should be finalized and approved *before* it goes to the art studio. No rewrites should be allowed after that point; those that are made will cost you more.

Desktop publishers and art studios generally bill AAs at an hourly rate above and beyond the project fee quoted, with the rate ranging from $40 to $75 or more per hour.

If you are proofreading the same document repeatedly, you may grow weary of reading it and let mistakes slip through. To sharpen your proofreading effectiveness, try proofreading the copy *backwards*. This slows you down and forces you to read one word at a time. Using this technique, you can often catch spelling errors you might otherwise have missed.

Have several people proofread the brochure at each stage. Do not rely on yourself or your writer for final proofreading. Both of you have seen the copy too many times to be totally effective proofreaders.

Hiring outside proofreaders is a good idea, especially on major brochure projects. Check your Yellow Pages or local writer's groups. The Editorial Free-lancers Association in New York City, phone (212) 929-5400, has a directory of its members, many of whom do editing and proofreading.

Preparing Photographs for the Printer

The graphic artist is responsible for this, but you should be aware of these basics:

Never write on the back or front of a photograph.   The impression made by your pen or pencil will show up as an unsightly streak or line in the printed brochure. Do not type captions on the backs of photos; the impact of the typewriter will affect reproduction quality.

Make sure the printer gets originals. Your printer needs original color slides or black-and-white prints. Reproductions made from reproductions have reduced sharpness and clarity.

Specify how much the photo is to be enlarged or reduced. This is indicated by percentage. Fifty percent means you want the printed image to be half the size of the original. Eighty percent means a reduction to four-fifths of the original size; 100 percent means the same size as the original; 150 percent indicates an enlargement one and a half times the size of the original; and 200 percent means an enlargement twice the size of the original.

Tell the printer how you want to crop the picture.   "Cropping" involves cutting out sections you don't want to appear in the printed piece. All cropping is done from the edges inward; you can't cut out part of the middle. The easiest way to tell the printer how you want a picture cropped is to make a photocopy, then draw lines on the photocopy indicating which portions are to be cropped off.

Label the photos to indicate their placement.   Although typography is pasted or printed directly on the mechanicals, original photos are not. Instead, the artist indicates the position of each photo by drawing and labeling boxes on the mechanical. Photo A goes in box A, and so on down the line. The easiest way to label your photographs is to write out a label on a piece of paper and tape it to the back of the photograph. With slides, you simply write the label notation on the frame.

If your artist has used desktop systems to produce your brochure and is equipped with an optical scanner, the photos can be scanned in and printed out directly on the proof along with the typeset copy.

You will hear artists refer to these proof pages as *FPO* or *for position only*. That means the photos are scanned in and placed on the page just to show the printer the correct position for photo placement. As discussed, the printer will need color transparencies or black-and-white prints for the actual printing of the piece.

Image Setting

Because of the cost of high-resolution output devices, most art studios and desktop publishing firms do not have the highest resolution output devices. For simple offset black-and-white fliers, letters, and other smaller projects, the output from a regular laser printer is sharp enough to be used as a mechanical and be reproduced directly on a printing press.

For about $800, you can buy a laser printer with a resolution of 300 dots per inch (dpi), good enough for producing camera-ready mechanicals for simple jobs. If you spend $1,500 to $2,000, you can get a better laser printer with twice that resolution. At 600 dpi, laser-printed text can be reproduced on a printing press with good-quality results. The resolution of the scanned-in photos, however, will still not be good enough for direct reproduction.

Service bureaus own expensive high-resolution image setters with four to eight times higher resolution than typical office or art studio laser printers. At these resolutions, black-and-white prints can be scanned into the computer system and printed in camera-ready form directly on the high-resolution printout. (Color printing is discussed below.)

The cost of high-resolution image setting is approximately $10 to $15 per page of text; more if halftones (photos) are involved. Ask any graphics or advertising people you know for the names of local service bureaus they use.

Must you or your artist use a high-resolution image setter to make camera-ready mechanicals if photos are involved? No. As discussed, most art studios have their own laser printers capable of producing camera-ready typeset brochure pages. Photos are scanned, or boxes are drawn FPO, to show the position of each visual.

Next, a *velox* is made of each black-and-white photo, using a special camera. Most printers and many art studios own the equipment needed to make veloxes and stats. The cost to produce veloxes or stats is approximately $5 to $15 apiece.

A *stat* is a reproduction of black-and-white artwork. A *velox* is a reproduction of a halftone.

In the velox process, the black-and-white print is shot through a screen that converts it from halftone into a series of dots. As you may know, printed matter consists of a series of dots of ink applied by a printing press to the paper. The higher the resolution (the more dots per inch), the better the quality of the printing.

The artist pastes the veloxes and stats into position on the camera-ready mechanical. Then the mechanical, after being checked and proofread using the checklist presented in Figure 9.1, is ready to be turned over to the printer for reproduction.

Mechanicals may be laser-printed on computer paper and given to the printer in that form, or the artist can paste up the type, veloxes, and stats onto cardboard. The stiff cardboard backing is less likely to be damaged in handling.

The artist will probably attach a tissue overlay (a thin, semitransparent sheet of tissue paper) over each board. This protects the mechanical from smudges and dirt. In addition, the artist can write instructions to the printer on the tissue overlay. For instance, if an illustration is to be printed in a certain color, the artist will indicate this in writing and will attach a sample swatch specifying the color in which the drawing is to be printed.

The standard system for specifying colors in printing is known as the *Pantone Matching System (PMS)*. Almost all printers and artists have swatch books showing the various PMS colors available and giving their number. Ask your printer or artist for a PMS color guide to keep in your office. This will help you select colors and communicate your choices to your vendors.

Figure 9.1 Checklist for proofreading your mechanical prior to its release to your printer.

Before you release the finished mechanical to the printer, ask yourself:

- ❒ Does it follow your approved layout? If not, why not?
- ❒ Are all logos, trademarks, registration marks, and other symbols properly sized, positioned, and typeset?
- ❒ Have all logos, trademarks, and proprietary product names been capitalized and given registration marks (®) or trademarks (TM) where appropriate?
- ❒ Have all disclaimers, standard paragraphs, and other fine print been placed in the appropriate position?

Figure 9.1 Continued.

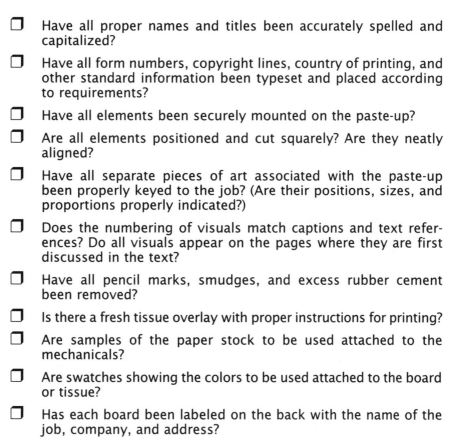

❏ Have all proper names and titles been accurately spelled and capitalized?

❏ Have all form numbers, copyright lines, country of printing, and other standard information been typeset and placed according to requirements?

❏ Have all elements been securely mounted on the paste-up?

❏ Are all elements positioned and cut squarely? Are they neatly aligned?

❏ Have all separate pieces of art associated with the paste-up been properly keyed to the job? (Are their positions, sizes, and proportions properly indicated?)

❏ Does the numbering of visuals match captions and text references? Do all visuals appear on the pages where they are first discussed in the text?

❏ Have all pencil marks, smudges, and excess rubber cement been removed?

❏ Is there a fresh tissue overlay with proper instructions for printing?

❏ Are samples of the paper stock to be used attached to the mechanicals?

❏ Are swatches showing the colors to be used attached to the board or tissue?

❏ Has each board been labeled on the back with the name of the job, company, and address?

Choosing Paper

Although you may have selected your paper earlier, you can still change your mind. Most printers have a wide selection of paper from which to choose. If they don't have a particular paper in stock, they can order it; however, ordering paper not in stock may delay the job. That's why you should order paper several weeks before you're ready to go to press—but only if you're absolutely certain about your choice.

Let your printer and graphic artist guide you in the selection of paper. Printers know, for example, which papers are best for showing off photos and which are best for taking up certain types of inks or coatings. Many times, they can save you money by suggesting a paper they can get at a discount from their special sources and suppliers.

Paper is graded by weight. Heavy papers are stiff and thick, lighter papers are thinner. Paper weight is measured in pounds (with the pound measurement referring to the weight of 500 sheets, not a single sheet). Newspapers are printed on 30-pound stock, résumés on 50- or 60-pound stock, magazines on 80- or 90-pound stock.

Another factor that affects stiffness is the thickness of the paper. Paper thickness is measured in *mils*; one mil is equal to one-thousandth of an inch.

Paper may be smooth and uniform in composition, or it may have an interesting weave or texture running through it. The surface may be dull, high-gloss, or somewhere in between. Paper is available in many variations of white and in an almost infinite variety of other colors.

Another consideration is *opacity*: Can you see through the paper when you hold it up to the light? Will ink printed on one side bleed through to the other? Opacity is determined by thickness, weight, and the manufacturing process and chemicals used to make the paper.

The most common grades of paper are as follows:

- *Bond papers* are used in stationery and business forms. Bond paper is easy to write on.

- *Text papers* have a rich texture and feel to them. They are used in booklets, brochures, and other print promotions.

- *Coated stock* has a glossy finish. It receives ink well and is the stock to use when you are reproducing color photographs in your literature. Coated stock is ideal for high-quality jobs, such as annual reports and corporate brochures.

- *Cover stock* is a heavier paper used mainly for brochure and booklet covers. It can be cut and embossed and stands up to heavy abuse. You can make your literature feel more substantial by printing the cover on cover stock and the inside pages on a lighter paper.

- *Book stock* is a less expensive grade of paper used, as its name implies, in books, including this one.

- *Offset paper* is similar to book stock and is used for résumés, cover letters, and other "quickie" printing jobs done on small offset presses.

Although it helps to know about paper, don't spend your time becoming an expert in the subject. Instead, lean on the expertise of your printer and artist and let them guide you.

Pick a grade of paper that does justice to the project. The look and feel of the paper determine, to a large extent, the first impression the reader receives from your literature. And first impressions, as you know, are important when it comes to doing business or making a sale.

One way of saving money is to buy paper in large quantities. Let's say you print a newsletter on a special gray-blue stock. Each issue has a press run of 5,000 copies, and you print six issues a year. Buy 30,000 sheets (one year's supply) at once instead of just 5,000. The savings will be substantial.

Another money-saving technique is to use paper the printer already has on hand. Since the printer loses money on paper he can't sell, you may get a better deal on existing inventory than if the printer has to order the paper especially for you. Also, many local printers often offer for sale the remainders of odd lots of paper. These sales allow you to buy perfectly good paper at incredibly low prices.

Selecting a Printer

Commercial printing today is a multibillion dollar industry, perhaps the largest industry in the country. And you will shortly be contributing to its profits.

Printing can account for between 25 and 75 percent of your production budget, and the cost of the job can vary by more than 30 percent from one printer to the next. Therefore, it pays to choose your printer with care. Here is some advice for doing it right:

■ Get a referral

The best way of finding potential printers for your job is through referral. Just about every organization uses the services of local printers at some point. Ask your associates at other firms to give you the names of two or three good printers they can recommend.

If referrals don't yield enough names, you can find numerous printers listed in the Yellow Pages. Also, printing is a competitive industry, so chances are that various local printers will mail you samples of their work or other direct mail in the hopes of soliciting your business. As you receive these mailings, file them away for future reference. Then, when the need for printing services arises, you will have a file full of suppliers right at your fingertips.

■ Use local printers

The printer should be located within a one-hour drive of your office. During the printing process, you will have to visit their facilities many times to check on the job and oversee the work. If the printer is far away, these visits can quickly eat up your time. Also, printers, like other professionals, must be compensated in some fashion for their time, and if they have to travel half a day to see you, they'll factor in this travel time when calculating your bill.

■ Go to the suburbs if necessary

As a rule, suburban and rural printers charge much less than printers located in major cities. The rural printer may be so far away that the cost savings isn't worth the extra time, so your best bet is a printer in a nearby suburb. The fee will be substantially less than that of a city printer, but if the printing plant is near a bus route or major highway, the extra travel time will be minimal.

■ Check out the operation in person

Don't just be content to meet with the printer's sales representative in your office or have them mail you some samples. Check them out carefully. Visit their facilities, have them explain their equipment and capabilities to you, and meet with the people who will be handling your job. Hire a printing firm whose people you feel you can trust with the important task of printing your publications correctly and on time.

■ Choose a specialist

Some printers specialize by type of project: annual reports, catalogs, direct mail. Others specialize according to printing process: offset, letterpress, gravure. A third group specializes according to the size of the run (the number of copies you need).

Choose a printer set up to handle your specific task. The advantage of using specialists is that they can often do a better job at significantly lower cost.

■ Get three bids

Once you've narrowed the field, select your three favorite printers and have them bid on the job. The information they'll need for an accurate price quotation includes the quantity to be printed, page size, number of pages, type of binding or folding, paper stock, colors, number of halftones, and deadline. The literature specification sheet you completed in Chapter 2 (Figure 2.3) will give printers all of this information and more. You should also give the printers a copy of your layout.

Getting three bids ensures that you pay a fair price for the job. If you solicited only a single bid, you would have no way of knowing whether it was reasonable or sky high. When you get three bids, you can immediately see whether a bid is out of line with what the others are charging.

■ Get it in writing

Insist on written proposals from your printers. The proposal should reiterate all of the specifications you've outlined along with the deadline, number of copies needed, and price for the job. A written agreement eliminates misunderstandings and protects you if the final bill is higher than the estimate or the job is not as you ordered it.

The Proof Stage

Bluelines

Once you hand over the mechanical to the printer, your work is nearly done. Here's what happens from that step on.

The printer's job is to reproduce your mechanical on a printing press. A printing plate is made. Then, before the copies are run from the plate, the printer gives you a *blueline* to check.

A blueline is a final proof of the work. It derives its name from the fact that it is printed as dark blue lettering on light blue photosensitive paper. The blueline gives you one final opportunity to proofread for typos and check for mistakes.

Take this opportunity. Occasionally, pieces of type fall off the mechanical or photos are placed upside down, and the printer does not notice. Proofing the blueline lets you catch and correct these mistakes before the job goes to press. Unfortunately, making changes at this stage is very expensive. You should also check the blues for broken type, splotches, smears, correct spacing, and correct placement of color (in two-color jobs).

After you approve the proofs, the printer duplicates the plates on the press. The pages are cut and folded or bound according to your instructions, and boxes of finished literature are shipped to you. And that's it.

Color separations

On full-color jobs, an additional step is involved: color separations. In a color separation, the original color picture is photographically or electronically separated into four basic colors: red, yellow, blue, and black. Each color is made into a halftone printing plate. When the four plates are printed on top of one another, the result is full, natural color reproduction.

For full-color reproduction of color photos in a printed piece, the printer should be given a slide or chrome if at all possible. The term *slide* refers to a color transparency in 35-millimeter format; any transparency shot using a larger format film is called a *chrome*.

If your artist has scanned color photos onto the mechanical electronically, they are FPO, for position only. The color transparencies must still be prepared for full-color reproduction on the printing press. This can be done in one of several ways.

One method is to take the color transparencies to a service bureau. The bureau will use a high-resolution image setter (known as a *drum scanner*) to scan in the transparencies at high resolution.

Or you can go to a printer or pre-press house equipped with a special image setter used to make color separations. The image setter converts the transparencies into digital form, then generates the separations.

Once the transparencies have been scanned, the drum scanner or pre-press image setter produces color separations, or films, from which the photos are to be reproduced. The films prepared for the printing press include all elements of each page of the brochure, copy, photos, and drawings.

As noted, full-color reproduction is made by using four inks—red, blue, yellow, and black—in different combinations. Therefore there will be four films, one for each color ink. (In a two-color printing job, by comparison, you would have just two films.)

In color work, you commonly proof what is known as a *color key*. The key consists of the four translucent sheets of film, each chemically treated with a pigment in one of the four basic colors. By placing the four sheets together, you see an image closely resembling what the final print will look like.

A more accurate (albeit slightly more costly) method of proofing color work is to make a *cromalin*, which uses a single sheet of paper instead of four acetate sheets. Cromalins have a much closer resemblance to the finished print than color keys.

If you are unhappy with the appearance of color photos in the keys or cromalins, tell this to the printer. Changes can be made by adjusting the application of the four basic colors of ink. However, the best way to ensure sharp color printing is to make your reproductions from high-quality color slide originals.

On major color jobs, you might also consider checking *press proofs* at the printing plant. A press proof is an actual printed version of the plates run as a final quality check prior to gearing up the presses for the full run. Some printing experts swear by press proofs; others feel they are not worth the expense and, in addition, are not a reliable method, because the press proof is often run on a different press than the final version will be.

If you are working with a printer specializing in four-color printing and you go to the plant to review a press proof, you will probably find that the room in which this is done is furnished and painted in gray. This is so that ambient colors and reflections do not affect your ability to view and judge the colors on the proof.

11 Tips on Getting Good Printing at Low Cost

1. Submit a perfect mechanical
A perfect mechanical is one the printer can work with directly without the need to clean it up, create additional artwork, or redo part of the mechanical. If the printer has to touch the mechanical because it's dirty, sloppy, or improperly prepared, you'll be charged extra for it.

2. Use the printer as a consultant
Get the printer's advice on what works and what doesn't. Involve the professional in the early stages of planning and design, not after the fact. The printer may be able to suggest alternative ways of designing and producing the piece, and these suggestions could save you a lot of money at press time.

3. Get great photographs
Photos should be sharp, clear, and full of contrast. If your photos are of poor quality, the printer can correct for that in the printing process—to a degree. But he won't make up the difference 100 percent. That's why good printing starts with good photography.

4. Submit transparencies

In color printing, better reproduction quality can usually be obtained working from slides rather than color prints. So use color slide film when you shoot, and submit original color slides to the printer.

And regardless of whether you're using slides or prints, color or black and white, submit originals, not copies. A *second-generation print* (reproduced from the original print rather than from the negative) will not reproduce as well as the original. A *third-generation print* (made from a second-generation print) is even worse. Reproduction quality declines in direct proportion to the generation of the print or slide.

5. Use full frames, not silhouettes

A silhouette is a visual in which a picture of an object is cut out of a photograph and reproduced as an outline figure using the white space of the page as background. Silhouettes add extra cost to the job. Using a regular product photo, one showing the product against the background in which it was photographed, is more economical.

6. Use basic colors

These are standard inks the printer stocks or can buy off the shelf. When you print in unusual colors, such as maroon or lavender, custom inks have to be mixed especially for your job, and that can increase printing costs by 15 to 25 percent or more.

7. Catch mistakes early

The earlier in the production process you catch mistakes, the easier and less costly they are to correct. So when you proof the mechanical, proof it carefully and try your best to eliminate all errors. Although you can make corrections if you spot typos in the blueline, it's expensive. Concentrate on your early proofing so your blueline will be letter-perfect.

8. Use a few large photos rather than many small ones

Try to use one large photo per page rather than many smaller ones. The reason? The fewer photos you use, the less the piece costs to produce. On average, each additional color photo will add $200 to $400 to the printing bill.

9. Print a large volume

Printing becomes more economical in larger volumes. Also, a large press run dramatically lowers your cost per piece. If you're not sure whether you'll need 5,000 or 10,000 pieces, order the 10,000. Having a few left over is much less costly than not printing enough and having to go back to press for an additional 5,000.

10. Fold smaller pieces

Folding is less costly than binding, so if you can form your brochure by folding one piece of paper into panels instead of binding several pieces of paper together, do so.

11. Take delivery at multiple sites

If your supply of literature is to be split among several locations, have the printer deliver the proper amount directly to each location. This is cheaper than having all the brochures sent to your office and then reshipping cartons to your various branch offices or dealers.

More cost-cutting tips

Galen Stilson, writing in *The Direct Response Specialist* (issue #79), gives these additional tips for cutting printing costs:

Choose the right process and printer. Short run versus long run, black and white versus color, and standard sheets versus specialty cuts all require different presses and processes. Make sure you choose a printer who has the right equipment for the job you need.

Combine jobs for one press run. You may be able to "gang print" two jobs on one press run and save money. Even on standard paper sizes, gang printing saves money.

For instance, for printing two 8½″ × 11″ inserts (2 sides, black ink on white 50 lb. offset paper), one printer quoted a charge of $212 for 5,000 of each. But for ganging the two inserts onto one 11″ × 17″ sheet, printing 5,000, and then having the printer cut the sheets into two 8½″ × 11″ pieces, the printer quoted a fee of $178.50. That's a 15 percent savings.

Give complete instructions. Don't expect your printer to guess what you want. Put your instructions in writing and make sure your printer understands.

Choose the right paper. If your job requires expensive linen stock, fine. But few do. And in those cases where you want your paper to have a feel to it, opt for less expensive paper with feel. Ask your printer.

Use screening to add color.   By screening or overprinting, you can create the illusion of multiple-color printing. Screening black to 20 percent gives you a distinctly different gray color.

Don't choose bleeds.   If you want your photos to bleed off the page (come right up to the edge of the paper), expect to pay more for this. Since bleeds seldom affect response, why waste the money?

Work closely with your printers.   You'll save money and anxiety.

Further Reading

A complete discussion of graphic arts techniques, procedures, and equipment is beyond the scope of this book. For more information on design, layout, paste-up, and printing, you can turn to the following reference books.

- *Graphic Arts Encyclopedia*, George A. Stevenson (New York: McGraw-Hill, 1992), 483 pages. A comprehensive reference work on creating and reproducing graphic images. Discusses the latest machinery, processes, and techniques.

- *Graphic Designer's Production Handbook*, Norman Sanders and William Bevington (New York, NY: Hastings House, 1982), 208 pages. Over 110 subjects covered, from preprinting preparation and halftone reproduction to lithography and finishing operations.

- *Graphics Master 5*, Dean P. Lem (Santa Barbara, CA: Dean Lem Associates, 1993). Covers a broad range of graphic arts topics including typography, computerized phototypesetting, proofreading, photography, halftone screens, color, papers, printing, binding, and finishing. Includes a glossary.

- *Mastering Graphics*, Jan V. White (New York: R. R. Bowker Co., 1983), 180 pages. A guide to design and production for people who publish newsletters, magazines, newspapers, tabloids, and internal corporate publications. Topics include logo design, masthead design, cropping and scaling halftones, and preparing mechanicals for printing.

- *Pocket Pal: A Graphic Arts Production Handbook* (New York: International Paper Company), 204 pages. This popular handbook was first published in 1934 and is now in its 12th edition. Chapters provide in-depth discussions of a wide range of graphics topics including printing methods, typesetting, copy and art preparation, photography, platemaking, binding, paper, and printing inks.

CHAPTER TEN

KEEPING IT GOING: HOW TO MANAGE A PROMOTIONAL LITERATURE PROGRAM

Opening a carton and pulling out a freshly printed, glossy booklet or brochure can be a very satisfying feeling, especially if you had a hand in its creation. But in most organizations, you can't rest on your laurels. At some point, the brochure will become dated, and you'll need a new one. Or else you'll have to produce additional literature to cover other areas or to supplement the original.

This chapter gives tips and advice on a miscellany of topics, all related to managing a successful program of promotional literature: You will get advice on how to generate customer interest in your literature; how to get salespeople and top management enthusiastic about your literature program; how to distribute, store, and reprint literature; how to create a successful series of brochures; and how to get the most out of existing copy, type, artwork, and photographs.

Selling Your Program to Top Management

Unless you're the boss, you need to convince top management to fund your literature program. Chances are, you will be required to submit some sort of promotional budget for approval. The budget outlines the projects you want to do and the money required for each.

If you've never done this before, and you expect to get instant approval for your ambitious plans, you're in for a shock: Management may, for example, think $8,000 is excessive for a brochure and cut that item to $2,500 ("Do we really need four-color illustrations?"). And projects you think of as essential may be eliminated altogether ("Let's use last year's brochure until sales go high enough to justify printing a new one").

Complaining that management doesn't understand the importance of good literature won't change their minds. Although they indeed may not understand the need for quality brochures, that lack of understanding is your problem, not theirs. It's your job to make them understand: to prove your case and defend your budget.

How do you get management to approve your budget and see your point of view? Here are some suggestions:

■ Educate your managers

Part of your job is to provide your management with an ongoing education in the value of advertising, publicity, and promotion. After all, they have many other things to worry about, and they may not spend as much time thinking about promotional literature as you do.

How do you educate management? One way is to read advertising and business magazines and clip any articles that pertain to promotional literature. Distribute copies of the articles, along with brief memos, to key managers.

Also, many printers, advertising agencies, and other vendors occasionally sponsor educational seminars or meetings for their customers. If you get invited, try to take some of your managers along. They'll gain an appreciation of what it takes to create a successful brochure or booklet.

■ Be cost-conscious

Some advertising and publicity directors, in their zeal to do a first-class job, are not as cost-conscious as they should be. Top management, on the other hand, is most impressed by a manager who can achieve goals as economically as possible, especially in today's economy.

Become cost-conscious and let your management know the steps you're taking to conserve promotional dollars. For example, if you prepare detailed cost estimates for each project, circulate these estimates to your managers. This will give your management a clearer picture of the expenses involved and will also show them that all budget requests are well thought out.

One technique to make the cost of producing literature seem more bearable is to state cost in terms of price per piece rather than price per project. Let's say it cost you $10,000 to produce a brochure and you printed 10,000 copies. Don't say the cost is $10,000. Say it is $1 per copy.

And, as I mentioned in the previous chapter, the cost of printing does not increase in direct proportion to the number of copies printed. Whereas a press run of 10,000 copies costs $10,000, a run of 20,000 copies might cost only

$12,000. By printing the extra copies, you lower your cost per copy to 60 cents, a figure that seems much more palatable on a budget sheet.

■ Track the competition

Collect samples of the competition's literature. Circulate these samples to your management. When management is aware of what the competition is doing, they'll be better able to appreciate why your own literature has to look at least as good. (They will also appreciate the effort you're making to gather valuable information on the competition's products and marketing efforts.)

■ Show the before and after

When you update or redo an old piece of literature, circulate the old brochure with the updated version. This side-by-side comparison dramatically demonstrates that the extra effort and cost involved in producing first-class literature pays off. Your management will immediately see, and appreciate, the difference in quality, image, and communications effectiveness. This will help pave the way for future efforts.

■ Get supporting opinions

If your customers and salespeople think highly of your literature, ask them to say so in writing. Then show these letters of praise to top management to prove the popularity of your new promotional efforts.

■ Demonstrate customer interest

Keep track of the number of brochures you distribute each year. Then, if management questions the effectiveness or need for literature, you can back up your claim that your brochure is in demand with a hard statistic (e.g., "2,400 requests for our catalog this year").

■ Measure effectiveness

Try to make some measurement of the brochure's readability, persuasiveness, and communications effectiveness. This is difficult but possible. (See the sections on Creating an Inquiry Fulfillment Package and Measuring Effectiveness later in this chapter.)

■ Divide the cost

If a project is too expensive for one department or division to fund, perhaps the cost can be shared by several groups within the organization. The annual report, for example, is used not only by the public relations department but also by marketing, sales, advertising, and human resources. Splitting the cost among various groups makes the price tag affordable to the managers of these divisions, who would hesitate to foot the whole bill themselves.

In the same way, you can make an art or photography budget seem more palatable if you can show how the cost can be spread over several projects. Five hundred dollars for pictures to be used in a slide presentation might seem excessive to some managers. But if you explain how the same photos will also be used in publicity, literature, and print advertising, the tight-fisted manager can see her or his way clear to approving your request.

Generating Enthusiasm Among Your Salespeople

If your organization sells its products or services through an inside sales force, sales reps, agents, distributors, or dealerships, a major application of your literature will be as a sales aid to support the efforts of your salespeople. It follows that the first step in creating successful promotional literature is to create literature that the salespeople will want to use. Gaining acceptance for your literature among the sales force begins in the planning stage, not after the fact.

Before you outline your brochure, talk to some of your dealers and salespeople. Find out what they think should be included in the literature—and what should be omitted. If you've already written an outline or draft, or have designed a rough layout, show it to your salespeople. Do they think the proposed brochure would be useful to them in their sales activities? Or do they complain that you're creating an expensive puff piece, a fancy but overly general brochure that fails to include any real information or sales talk?

Take these criticisms and complaints for what they're worth. You don't have to agree with every comment. But remember: The salespeople are the ones who have to go out and sell the product on a daily basis. They can give you a lot of guidance about what sells—and what doesn't. Incorporate the best of their thinking into the finished piece.

If you follow this procedure, you'll gain speedy acceptance of your literature by salespeople for two reasons. First, the literature will reflect their need for an effective sales support tool. And second, they'll appreciate the fact that you took the time to consult with them on the project.

Be sure to distribute an adequate supply of literature to all branch offices, dealerships, manufacturer's representatives, and inside salespeople. Let them know that additional copies are available and make it easy for them to request these extra copies.

Keep in touch with the sales force so you can get feedback on your literature's success. Experience in using the literature may provide additional ideas on how to improve it for the next press run. For example, maybe you didn't include certain information because you thought it was unimportant, but your salespeople report that every customer is asking for that information. In the next edition, you might highlight that information up front.

Publicizing Your Brochure

Is the publication of your new catalog or brochure news? Not to the *New York Times* or the *Wall Street Journal,* perhaps. But there are many specialty publications whose readers want to know about the availability of your new literature.

Press releases

One way to publicize the publication of new promotional literature is with a *new-literature release.* This is simply a short press release announcing the publication and availability of your new brochure, catalog, booklet, or handbook.

The new-literature release begins with a headline announcing the publication. The text of the release describes the contents of the literature in a way that makes it most interesting to editors and their readers. The closing paragraph explains how the reader can obtain a free copy of the publication being discussed. The press release is typed double-spaced and is usually a page long, two pages at most. A typical new-literature release is shown in Figure 10.1.

Figure 10.1 Sample press release publicizing new promotional literature.

<u>FROM</u>: Kirsch Communications, 226 Seventh St., Garden City, NY 11530. For more information please call: Len Kirsch, 516/248-4055

<u>FOR</u>: Globe Electronic Hardware, Inc., 32-02 57th St., Woodside, NY 11377. Contact: Patrick J. Dennehy, President, 212/278-2400

For immediate release

GLOBE OFFERS NEW CATALOG

FOR ELECTRONIC HARDWARE

A new 188-page catalog containing complete engineering dimensions, specifications, materials, and finishes for its entire line of electronic hardware components has been published by Globe Electronic Hardware, Inc., Woodside, NY.

According to Patrick J. Dennehy, president, the new catalog provides new and revised data for all of the company's standard products, rearranged for easier selection and specification by design engineers. Products featured include....[description of products]

Copies of the catalog are available without charge from John Choberka, Globe Electronic Hardware, Inc., 32-02 57th Street, Woodside, NY 11377, telephone 1 (800) 221-1505 or (212) 278-2400.

###

Note to editor: Cover photo, copy of catalog enclosed

Do editors print these releases? The answer is yes, many do. There are thousands of specialty magazines covering every conceivable field, from agriculture and aerospace to television broadcasting and industrial training. *Bacon's Publicity Checker* is a book listing these thousands of magazines. It is published by Bacon's Publishing Company, 14 East Jackson Blvd., Chicago, IL 60604, (312) 922-8419. The reference room of your local library probably has a copy on its shelves.

The press release is typed, reproduced (by offset printing or as clear photocopies), and mailed to any magazine or newspaper that might have an interest in it. Your local paper probably won't be interested in your new ball-bearing catalog, but the readers of *Machine Design, Design News, New Equipment Digest*, and other journals aimed at design engineers would be very interested in obtaining the catalog. The editors, knowing this, may very well publish a short feature item describing your catalog. Some editors like to illustrate these items with a picture of the literature, so you should include the actual catalog or a photo of its cover with your release.

When the release is published, people will read it and many will send for a free copy of your brochure. In this way, publicity generates sales leads at practically no cost, because you do not pay the magazine to run your release.

Direct mail

Direct mail is another vehicle that is effective in generating requests for your literature.

How do you go about it? First, obtain a list of the names and addresses of qualified prospects, people who would be interested in your product and should receive a copy of your brochure. The best list is probably your customer list. Second-best is your list of prospects, people who have shown interest in your products or organization but have not yet made a purchase. Third-best is a list compiled by another organization and rented to you for mailing purposes. You can rent such lists from trade journals (subscription lists), professional societies (membership lists), trade shows (attendee lists), and special companies known as "list brokers." Many list brokers advertise their services on the pages of *Direct Marketing* magazine, 224 Seventh Street, Garden City, NY 11530, (516) 746-6700.

Next, create the direct-mail piece. The simplest format is a one- or two-page typewritten letter and reply card mailed in an ordinary business envelope.

If you have a word processor and the list is available on floppy disk, you might want to personalize your mailing. But if you don't have a computer and computerized list, you will probably have to make do with a form letter. That's okay, because form letters can still be extremely effective.

Outside print shops and *letter shops* (firms specializing in direct mail) can also produce personalized direct mail for you. But this is not usually economical for mailings of under 5,000 letters.

The letter highlights the benefits of the product and urges the reader to send for the free brochure by completing and mailing the reply card. Each reply card you receive represents a hot sales lead, someone with immediate interest in your product.

Sending out direct mail is more expensive than writing a press release, but it is also more of a sure thing. With a press release, there is no guarantee that an editor will run it, hence no guarantee that your message will reach your prospects. But with direct mail, you have precise control over who receives your mailing. Also, by mailing only to qualified prospects, you generate a higher quality sales lead than you would with editorial publicity, which reaches a more diverse audience.

The key to getting the best response to your mailing is to concentrate on the offer of the free literature rather than on the product or service itself. Here's a sample letter designed to get the reader to send for a free pamphlet on "Life Insurance for Children."

There's no gift
more meaningful...

...for the children you love, than the one discussed in a new free pamphlet. It is yours with my compliments if you'll just mail the card enclosed.

You'll be surprised at the gift, I am sure. Most people are—at first. For that gift is "Juvenile Life Insurance."

Before you object that children rarely die young and so life insurance is depressingly inappropriate, let me surprise you again by saying that people invest in life insurance for children precisely because they expect these children to *live*!

But you'll appreciate the good sense of this with this informative pamphlet in your hands. Just complete and mail the card and it's yours...

[list of product benefits as described in the pamphlet]

The free pamphlet contains the little-known facts. You my decide against this gift, of course. But I am sure you'll want to know why so many millions of devoted men and women do give this gift—every single year. Please complete and mail the card—and see.

Sincerely,

Integrating Literature and Advertising

A powerful technique for increasing the response to your advertisements is to offer free literature to people who respond to the ad. To take advantage of this technique, your advertising agency or department must be kept informed about the promotional literature you have available immediately, as well as the pieces you're planning to publish in the near future.

Here are some tips on how to use your print advertising to generate interest in your literature:

Use your closing paragraphs of ad copy to describe the booklet. Example: "To get the full story on our complete line of hobbyist telescopes and accessories, phone or write for a free copy of our new, full-color booklet and product directory, *A Layman's Guide to the Stars*."

Make your booklet sound useful. People are more likely to request a booklet that contains useful advice and tips as opposed to a brochure that is purely a sales pitch. Include some useful information of a general nature in your literature. By stressing the informative aspect of your booklet, you'll generate more inquiries.

Give the literature an attractive title. The title should imply value and make people want to have a copy. For example, if your pump catalog gives tips on product selection, call it a *pump selection guide* instead of a *pump catalog*. The word *guide* implies helpful advice and information, whereas *catalog* sounds more like a blatant sales pitch.

Use a coupon in your ad layout. A coupon increases response by 25 to 100 percent. The coupon belongs in the bottom right-hand corner of the ad. It should be large enough so the reader can fill in the required information (name, address, phone number).

Use a toll-free number. Clipping a coupon takes effort. Many people do not have stamps and envelopes handy. A toll-free number provides a quick and easy way for people to request your literature.

Show a picture of the booklet. Don't make it the central visual, of course. But showing a photo of the booklet at the bottom right-hand corner, near the closing copy, will increase response. Put a caption under the photo to highlight the value of the literature. For example: "20-page color catalog of telescopes and accessories—yours *FREE*."

Don't try any funny business. People are wary of trickery. Be sure to stress that the booklet is sent free with absolutely no obligation on the part of the consumer.

Don't mention any follow-up. If you plan to follow up your mailing with a phone call or visit by a salesperson, do not mention this in your ad copy. Saying that a salesperson will call drastically reduces response.

Note: Make sure your literature copy is consistent with your ad copy. If you create a new ad campaign based on a service theme, and your existing product literature doesn't mention service, you may need to revise the literature or create a separate piece to highlight the service capabilities.

Creating an Inquiry Fulfillment Package

Naturally, you're not in business to publish free brochures and mail them. The purpose of generating inquiries and fulfilling them is to bring you one step closer to making a sale. But too many times, the mailing of the brochure does not lead to a sale. Instead, the brochure is thrown away, and a hot sales lead quickly turns cold.

Why? Part of the reason is that the brochure alone is not enough to move the prospect to action. You need more than just a brochure, you need a complete *inquiry fulfillment package*.

An inquiry fulfillment package is used to respond to leads generated by advertising, direct mail, publicity, and other promotions. It consists of a group of coordinated materials designed to hook the prospect's interest, provide the requested information, and bring about the next step in the buying process. These materials include:

■ **Outer envelope**

Even the design of the envelope the brochure is mailed in has an effect on whether the prospect reads the enclosed material or throws it away (See Figure 10.2). An envelope used for mailing inquiry fulfillment materials should be imprinted with the words "Here is the information you requested" or a similar message. This alerts the recipient that the envelope contains material that was requested, rather than the type of unsolicited advertising matter that is often referred to as junk mail.

■ **Brochure**

"The proper literature—what the respondent is asking for—is the most important part of the package," says Larry Whisenhant, advertising manager of Koch Engineering, a manufacturer of chemical equipment. The fulfillment package should include all of the material the prospect requested along with any additional literature that can answer questions or help make the sale.

Figure 10.2   When mailing literature in response to an inquiry, imprint the envelope with a message to alert readers that the envelope contains information they requested—and not unsolicited direct mail.

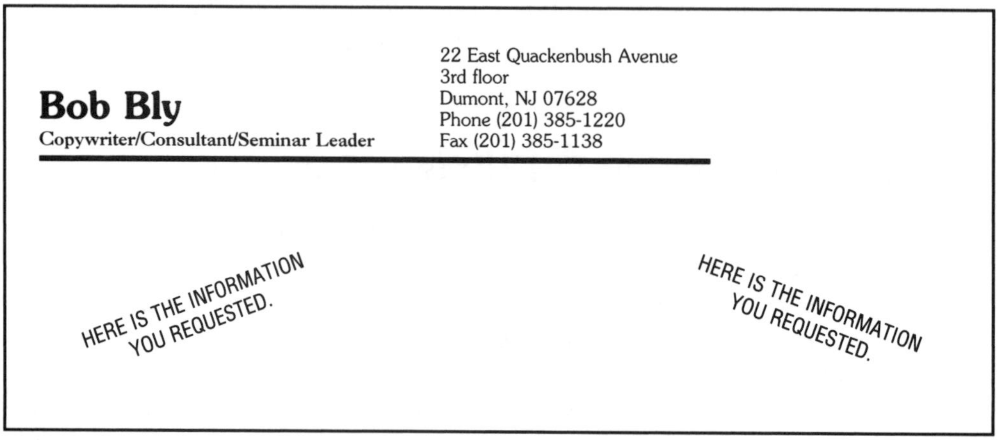

Bob Bly
Copywriter/Consultant/Seminar Leader

22 East Quackenbush Avenue
3rd floor
Dumont, NJ 07628
Phone (201) 385-1220
Fax (201) 385-1138

HERE IS THE INFORMATION YOU REQUESTED.

HERE IS THE INFORMATION YOU REQUESTED.

■Reply element

The reply element is a device the reader can use to initiate the next step in the buying process, whatever that step may be. It can be a reply card, an order form, a questionnaire, or a specification sheet.

The most common reply element is the business-reply postcard. On the back of the card is space for the prospect to fill in her or his name, address, and phone number. There are also boxes to check that indicate the recipient's level of interest.

The front of the card contains your name and address and a postage-paid business reply permit number. The prospect simply completes the card and tosses it in the mail—no need to add postage. The card comes back to you, and you take the appropriate action.

■ Dealer list

Most people prefer to buy from a local store, agent, or dealer rather than direct from the manufacturer. If you use local dealers, agents, or outlets, the fulfillment package should supply the prospect with the name, address, and specific location of the nearest dealer.

There are several ways to handle this. One is to include a cover letter signed by the local dealer and written on the dealer's letterhead. Another way is to have a cover letter from the manufacturer only but to attach the dealer's business card or give the dealer's name and address in the text of the letter. A third way is to print a listing of all dealers and include it with the inquiry fulfillment package. Such a listing is best organized by state, city, or zip code. And you can circle the name of the appropriate dealer in red pen to make it even easier for the prospect to find.

Finally, you can produce personalized inquiry fulfillment letters one at a time on your PC, inserting the prospect's name at top and the name and phone number of the local dealer in the body or "cc" of the letter.

■ Cover letter

The cover letter ties the package together. The literature concentrates on selling the product, but the cover letter concentrates on telling the reader about the next step in the buying process—and on urging her or him to take it (See Figure 10.3).

A good cover letter starts by thanking the prospect for having interest in your product. Next, it highlights specific product benefits or gives a brief overview of the enclosed literature. Then it describes the next step in the sales cycle. Finally, it closes by urging the reader to take action.

Figure 10.3   Here's an excellent example of an effective cover letter for an inquiry fullfillment package:

Dear Mr. Moore,

Thanks for your interest in our Pelletizers. Literature is enclosed which will give you a pretty good idea of the simplicity of our equipment and its rugged, trouble-free construction.

The key question, of course, is the cost for equipment to handle the volume at your plant. Since the capacity of our Pelletizers will vary slightly with the particulates involved, we'll be glad to take a look at a random 5-gallon sample of your material. We'll evaluate it and get back to you with our equipment recommendation. If you will note with your sample the size pellets you prefer and the volume you wish to handle, we can give you an estimate of the cost involved.

From this point on we can do an exploratory pelletizing test, a full day's test, or we will rent you a production machine with an option to purchase. You can see for yourself how efficiently it works and how easy it is to use. Of course the equipment can be purchased outright, too.

Thanks again for your interest. We'll be happy to answer any questions for you. Simply phone or write.

Very truly yours,

MARS MINERAL CORPORATION

All five elements—envelope, literature, reply element, dealer list, and cover letter—work together to create a cohesive sales tool. The best way to put the package together is to mail the literature and letter flat in a 9" × 12" (or larger) envelope. The letter is the first thing the reader should see when pulling your materials out of the envelope. Underneath the letter is the literature, followed by the reply element. You may want to clip the materials to a piece of stiff cardboard to prevent the package from being folded, bent, or otherwise mutilated in the mail.

Tracking Your Sales Leads

You will need to devise an inquiry fulfillment and management system to keep track of inquiries and sales leads. The system should allow you to track the following information:

- Number of inquiries generated by each ad, mailer, press release, or other promotion
- Source of each individual inquiry
- Name, address, and phone number of each prospect
- Specific literature sent to each prospect and on what date
- Nature and date of follow-up contacts—mailings, phone calls, sales visits
- Facts about each prospect such as budget, level of interest, specific application
- Whether the inquiry resulted in a sale, is still pending, or can be considered inactive (because the prospect lost interest or bought from somebody else)

You can devise any inquiry tracking system that suits you. It can be computerized or manual.

In my own free-lance copywriting and consulting business, I use a manual system. It consists of two notebooks used to track inquiries. The first notebook is a record of the various ads and promotions I've tried, along with the results. For each promotion, it lists the date, a general description, the number of responses, and the amount of business generated, if any.

The second notebook uses a standard form to keep track of individual leads (See Figure 10.4). I keep a separate sheet on each prospect, and the book is divided into sections for "prospects ready to buy," "hot leads," "follow-up required," "cold leads," "inactive prospects," and "past customers." The form I use for tracking leads is reprinted below. You can easily adapt it to your own requirements.

Figure 10.4 Form for tracking leads.

Date _____ Source of inquiry: _____

Method of response: _____

NAME _____ TITLE _____

COMPANY _____ PHONE _____

ADDRESS _____

CITY _____ STATE _____ ZIP _____

Type of business: _____

Services required: _____

STATUS:

(   ) Sent literature on (date): _____

(   ) Enclosed these materials: _____

(   ) The next step is to: _____

(   ) Probability of closing the sale: _____

(   ) Date of next contact: _____

(   ) COMMENTS: _____

_____

CONTACT RECORD:

Date: Summary of conversation:

Using a detailed form such as this one allows you to precisely track the status of each lead. By doing so, you have a better chance of converting more leads into sales. Of course, the more inquiries you receive, the more difficult it is to keep track of them all. That's why many organizations have computerized their inquiry management systems.

The computerized system uses software and a personal computer to take the place of paper forms and notebooks. The advantage of computerization is that the computer is far more flexible and versatile than paper systems.

You can, for example, instruct the computer to print out an alphabetical list of prospects who requested "bulletin X" within the last six months, or to erase from the files all leads received more than three years ago. The computer can print reports, customized cover letters, and self-stick mailing labels. By tapping a few keys, you can call up any one of a thousand or more customer files in less than a minute. And you can easily change or update a file at any time.

How can you obtain a computerized inquiry management system? You can have a staff or independent computer programmer create one for you. Or you can buy one of a number of packaged systems that come complete and ready to go. Some of these consist of hardware and software installed in your office; others are computerized inquiry fulfillment services that are performed for you off-premises. Some of the best known include:

Automated Sales Support System
Epsilon Data Management, Inc.
24 New England Executive Park
Burlington, MA 01803
(617) 273-0250; (800) 225-1919

DCS
Dynatron Computer Systems, Inc.
127 W. 30th St.
New York, NY 10001
(212) 947-1212

ISA
Inquiry Systems Analysis
35 Morrissey Blvd.
Boston, MA 02125
(617) 482-6256

LCS Lead Conversion System
LCS Industries
120 Brighton Rd.
Clifton, NJ 07012
(201) 778-5588

The Order Prospector
Marketing Applications Software Company
5963 Tulane Street
San Diego, CA 92122
(619) 453-8758

Pending Business Reporting System
SMS Sales Management Systems
50 Church Street
Cambridge, MA 02138
(617) 492-1571

Prospecting
Key Systems, Inc.
512 Executive Park
Louisville, KY 40207
(502) 897-3332

Qualified Lead System
McGraw-Hill
1221 Avenue of the Americas
New York, NY 10020
(212) 997-3413

Quantum
Computer Marketing Services
1895 Mt. Hope Avenue
P.O. Box 1011
Rochester, NY 14603
(716) 271-2500

The Sales Manager
Market Power Computer Innovations
11780 Rough & Ready Road
Rough & Ready, CA 95975
(916) 432-1200

You can also "outsource" your inquiry handling and literature fulfillment to a third-party firm that provides such services. Ask colleagues for the name of fulfillment houses they use. One large inquiry handling and fulfillment house is ADH in Edison, New Jersey, phone (908) 417-5600; ask for Tom Costner. Another is the Fulfillment Center in Passaic, New Jersey, phone (201) 471-1111. From experience, I can also recommend Fala Direct Marketing in Melville, New York, phone (516) 694-1919. Ask for Bub Jurick and tell him I sent you.

Setting Up Your Literature Center

When an organization begins a literature program, an unlucky administrative assistant is usually selected to handle the mailing, stocking, and reordering of brochures. As your literature program grows, one employee working on inquiry fulfillment part-time can't hope to keep up with the leads. At some point, you realize that you need to set up a separate area to handle the task.

This literature center can be a separate room or the corner of an office. It can require the services of a single worker or a team working full-time stuffing envelopes and entering leads into the computer, depending on your volume. The important thing is to make the distribution and management of literature a separate function, and not something your secretary or clerk does when he or she has some extra time.

Here are some things to consider when setting up your literature center:

Space.   Have a completely separate room or area set aside for the task. Don't ask a secretary or group of secretaries to do the job in their normal workspace. They will quickly run out of room and become overwhelmed. Handling and mailing multiple pieces of literature takes space.

How big should your literature center be? Estimate the space you need to handle your current volume and multiply by two. That's the minimum area you'll need to handle your current and future volume. When estimating space requirements, consider all the things you'll need for your literature center. These may include shelving, space for boxes, desks and chairs, a cabinet for storing office supplies, a computer (if you use a computerized inquiry management system, a postage meter, and a place to keep outgoing mail until the mail carrier arrives.

Location.   Since there will be a steady flow of mail into and out of the literature center, try to locate it near your mail room or some other point convenient to the post office or assigned mail pick-up spot. Don't force employees to drag or cart heavy bundles of outgoing literature to a distant location for sorting and mailing.

Supplies.   Determine how many people will work in the literature center at the same time. Then put in at least two additional desks or tables. Promotional activities vary seasonally, and you should have space for temporary help when things get busy. Also, flat surfaces are helpful for organizing fulfillment materials and activities.

Set up the literature center as a pleasant, efficient workplace. Workers should have everything they need within easy reach. If, for example, literature is to be bound into spiral or hard-spine notebooks, keep the binding machine in the literature center. Make sure the people can do their work with the least amount of movement and travel. A postage meter is a worthwhile investment. It will keep a running total so you know your postage costs for inquiry fulfillment.

Stock the literature center with an ample supply of all essential items. In addition to an inventory of promotional literature, these can include envelopes, stamps, cardboard backings, paper clips, rubber bands, mail bags, address labels, form letters, notebooks, forms, pencils, pens, and computer supplies.

Storage.   Equip the literature center with shelves for stocking an ample supply of brochures. The best shelves are the metal type found in warehouses. Shelving allows workers to quickly find and pull the material they need. Do not store your working supply of literature in boxes, this makes the material hard to get at.

Shelves, of course, hold a limited supply and have to be restocked at intervals. The bulk of your inventory is best stored in the original cardboard boxes in which it arrived from the printers. Be sure the literature center has enough room to stock these boxes. Stocking boxes against a wall in a large, open room is best because it allows easy access. A cramped closet makes it difficult to find and open the boxes you need. Avoid storing boxes of literature in basements or other areas where printed material will be exposed to excess moisture.

The room should be dry, well-lit, and kept at normal room temperature. Excess humidity and extreme temperature changes can cause printed material to wrinkle and fade.

Ideally, one or more employees should work in the literature center full-time. If workers complain that this is boring, you could rotate assignment to the literature center among available clerical personnel.

The main idea behind all this is to process leads and get the literature in the mail quickly and efficiently. Hot leads can cool off fast, and the longer you sit on your inquiries, the more business you lose. Speed is of the essence when it comes to turning leads into sales. Inquiries should be fulfilled within 48 hours.

Expanding Your Literature Program

As your organization grows, so will your need for literature. Many large companies have dozens of different publications an all facets of their business. Even many small organizations have multiple brochures or booklets. There are two basic reasons to create and publish additional bulletins. The first is to explain something that isn't covered in current publications. The second is because you feel the new brochure or booklet can help you promote your product, program, or cause more effectively than a single booklet can. Here are some situations that may warrant publication of a new piece:

You have a new product.   Your prospects need to be informed of new products, new services, new accessories, new options, and new models. Sales literature is often the best medium for keeping your prospects informed of the latest developments.

Your product has new applications.   If you uncover a new application for an existing product, you may want to create a new brochure showing how the product can be used in this application.

You discover a new market. The best way to reach a group of prospects is to talk about their problems in their language. If you uncover a new potential market for your product, you may need a new piece of literature aimed at this specific market.

You begin to target communications. Maybe your brochure doesn't address the needs and interests of various buyers as strongly as it should. The solution might be to create separate pieces of literature aimed at specific audiences (top management, purchasing agents, wholesalers, retailers, consumers).

You have a new message. Perhaps you want to say something new about your business. Old literature must be revamped, or new literature created, to get this message across to your audience.

You have new case histories. Every product success story is another piece of ammunition in your arsenal of sales and marketing weapons. You can publish new bulletins on case histories you feel are noteworthy or of special interest to your customers.

You have new information. Have you come up with a better way to use, select, size, fix, or maintain your product? Has your organization or someone in it done something that is especially newsworthy or exciting? You may need to regularly publish new literature to provide your audience with a steady stream of information, ideas, advice, and news. A newsletter is often the best vehicle for accomplishing this.

Deciding Which Brochure Projects Are Worthwhile

If your organization is typical, you won't have to go searching for opportunities to produce more literature. Rather, once your people see how useful your first brochure is, they'll come begging for more. You'll be bombarded with requests to produce all sorts of materials for a wide variety of top executives, salespeople, managers, divisions, branch offices, dealers, and departments.

Sounds great—until you stop to consider that each new brochure takes time and money to produce. Since both of those resources have their limits, you must be selective in the projects you take on. You can produce *some* of those new brochures this year, but not all of them.

The merits of each proposed project must be evaluated, and you and your management team must come to a decision on which to proceed with and which to put on hold. Here are some of the questions you should ask when evaluating whether a suggested project is really worth pursuing:

■ **Is the topic covered elsewhere?**

Check to see what you've already published on the subject. You may find that a particular topic is already covered adequately in your current literature. Perhaps you can even reprint a page from your current brochure or catalog as a separate flier instead of going through the expense and effort of creating an entirely new piece from scratch.

■ **Does the subject really need its own vehicle?**

Does the topic really need its own piece of literature? Or can it be absorbed into, or combined with, another publication? A number of minor case histories, for example, can be featured in the company newsletter instead of published as stand-alone bulletins. A product accessory can be adequately marketed by including it in the product brochure or catalog instead of creating a separate flier for it.

■ **Is there enough interest?**

When someone comes to you with a request to create a new piece of literature, ask: "How many copies will you need?" The answer tells you whether the audience is large enough to justify the cost and expense. Any literature more elaborate than a one-page flier probably cannot be printed economically in a press run of under 1,000.

■ **Is the project important enough?**

A product with annual sales of $450 doesn't justify the cost of a $25,000 color brochure. The bulk of your promotional dollars should go to backing your winners, not your losers. It is not worth your while to produce literature on products that don't sell. Many managers don't think twice about putting in a request for a new brochure. They do not realize the time and money that it takes to produce quality literature. If they did, they wouldn't make their requests so lightly. Educate your management as to the cost, time, and effort involved in each new project. This will cause them to be more selective in their requests for new literature.

Your printer, artist, or ad agency can quickly give you a rough estimate of the cost of the proposed literature. Do you have enough money in the budget to pay for it? Assuming you do, are you willing to spend that much? Also, remember that money is a limited resource; the launching of one project usually means that some other project will have to be put on hold. Consider the relative importance of each proposed piece, and then set priorities.

■ **Do you have the time?**
The person responsible for supervising the literature program has limited time. So does her or his staff, and there is a limit to the number of projects you can tackle in a year. Again, consider the importance of each project and set priorities. Do not take on more work than time allows. If you don't have time to complete essential projects, make greater use of outside vendors and consider hiring more inside help.

■ **Is there a more effective marketing alternative?**
Promotional literature isn't always the answer to a marketing problem. Perhaps some other type of communication—a print ad, a press release, a speech, a sales letter, a videotape, a telemarketing campaign, an invoice stuffer—can solve the problem more effectively. Don't immediately rush into a brochure project without first considering the alternatives.

Measuring Effectiveness

In direct mail, you can scientifically measure the mailing's success by counting the number of orders or leads it generates. But measuring the effectiveness of literature is more difficult: Literature is only part of the sales and marketing effort; therefore, it is harder to isolate its contributions to the sale.

Still, it is helpful to be able to have some measure of a brochure's success or failure in the marketplace. Here are a few ways of making these measurements:

Get opinions.   Ask select customers and salespeople to write a short letter giving their opinion of your new literature program. Then carefully review what they've written. Their comments, although not a scientific measure of effectiveness, can give you a lot of insight into how your literature is being received in the marketplace.

Keep distribution records.   Counting the number of brochures you distribute each year will give you a rough measure of how interested people are in obtaining them.

Survey brochure recipients.   Develop a questionnaire and survey a random sampling of prospects and customers by mail or phone. Ask if they received the literature, if they read it, if they remember it. Quiz them on specific facts to determine how well they remember it. Ask their opinion of its format, usefulness, readability, and appearance. Tally the results and see what conclusions you can draw.

Build in a reply element and measure returns.   Let's say, for example, that the next step the reader should take after reading the brochure is to phone for an appointment with a salesperson. You could put a special code in the copy (e.g., "ask for Department 16") so you can determine how many incoming phone calls are a direct result of the brochure. The same technique can work for mail inquiries. Have the reader write to "Department 16" or some other key address so you can measure which inquiries are a direct result of the brochure. If you bind reply cards into literature, code the cards so you know which piece of literature a particular card came from. This device gives you a crude tool for measuring the response to your literature. It is not a perfect tool— brochures do much more than just generate leads—but at least it gives you some idea of how many people have been moved to action by your literature.

Include a tear-out survey or questionnaire.   Have the printer perforate the page so it is easily removed. Forms can be mailed or faxed back to you. A significant number of forms returned indicates people are reading through the brochure and taking the time to qualify themselves as prospects. Figure 4.3 shows such a reply element from a brochure describing a consulting service.

Merchandising Your Literature

To *merchandise* a promotion means to get maximum exposure out of it by using it again and again, in many shapes and forms.

For instance, when a newspaper or magazine publishes an article about a company, the article gives the company free, and hopefully favorable, publicity. But the publicity is over once the article is printed—unless you merchandise it.

How can you merchandise an article? Well, the first step is to get reprints. The reprints can be handed to customers by salespeople and made available as reading material in the company's reception area. By circulating reprints, you gain a wider audience for the article than just the readers of the magazine in which it was published.

But don't stop there. You could create a direct-mail package consisting of the article reprint with a cover letter. The article could also serve as the basis for an advertisement. Perhaps it could be reprinted in the annual report. You can begin to see how, with merchandising, a single promotion does double and triple duty and more.

You can also merchandise the elements of your printed promotions (copy, artwork, illustrations, photos). And this is a great way to stretch your literature budget.

Let's say you are producing a new brochure on product X. You want to take new photographs of product X for the brochure, but are shocked to discover that the cost of hiring a first-rate photographer for the day is $900.

Perhaps $900 is excessive for this one brochure. But stop to consider how much mileage you can get out of this photo session. You can use the photos in so many other promotions: slide presentations, press releases, trade show panels, the company newsletter, the annual report. Spread over all of these projects, the cost seems much more reasonable.

Copy can also be merchandised. You may, for example, pay a top copywriter $1,000 to write a corporate ad. But this copy, with minor modification, can be used as the introduction to the annual brochure or as corporate "boilerplate" (a standard, approved written description of the company used in all printed literature). If you run the ad copy in 10 different bulletins, the cost is only $100 per bulletin.

Look for ways to merchandise existing artwork, illustrations, photography, and copy. You'll save a bundle.

Here's one additional tip: You can also save money by using rejected art and copy for other projects. For example, your copywriter may submit five headlines before you find one you like for your new advertisement. Save those other headlines, maybe they can be used in other ads, on the cover of a brochure, or as the opening of a direct-mail piece.

In the same way, if you hire a photographer for a day, be sure the fee entitles you to keep the negatives of the entire day's work. Photos that you rejected for your new color brochure may be perfectly suitable for a quickie flier, a press release, or a newsletter. Note: Not all photographers will agree to such an arrangement.

Storing Artwork, Photos, and Mechanicals

Artwork, mechanicals, films, and printing plates must be stored safely. Careless handling can, in a second, ruin months of costly work.

The best place to store your films or printing plates is with the printer, who has the space and facilities to store them safely. And orders for reprints can be filled faster if your plates are already on the premises. Also, the printer will guarantee the condition of film and plates he or she stores, but relinquishes responsibility once you take the plates with you.

Mechanicals and artwork should be stored flat on shelves or, better yet, in special cabinets designed for storing artwork. Do not pile mechanicals too high or the weight will bend the boards. Also, high stacks are likely to fall over, and mechanicals can be damaged in the fall.

When storing mechanicals and art, make sure the surface of the board is protected with tissue overlays. If the overlays are missing or frayed, your artist can put on new ones. You might also enclose each board in a manila envelope for added protection.

If your brochure was produced electronically, then the best way to store the copy and layout is on disk. With the entire brochure—graphics and text—on disk, it's easy and inexpensive to revise and update your literature; you can make changes yourself without paying additional fees to an outside artist. Be sure to back up computer files on a floppy disk or tape.

Photo prints and negatives can be stored in ordinary manila file folders. Photo files should be arranged alphabetically, by subject. Never use paper clips to attach labels (or anything else) to photographs.

Slides can be stored in special plastic sheets. These sheets clip into three-ring binders. Special slide cabinets provide an even better way of storing slides. In these, slides are stored on a series of vertical metal racks that pull out for easy access. Many cabinets also have a pull-out lighted panel to illuminate the slides. Be sure to mark on the frame of the slide which slides are originals and which are duplicates. For security, you may want to keep originals in a separate place.

Numbers and Codes

A special code, printed in tiny type on the back page of your literature, can be a great help in managing your literature program. For starters, the code clearly identifies each separate piece. Let's say your company is called Clarkson Industries and you manufacture power tools. The first brochure on your new power drill might be coded CPD—B1, for "Clarkson Power Drill, Brochure #1." If you print a new version, it would be coded CPD-B2, for Brochure #2.

You can also use codes to indicate the publication date of the brochure. The code 0194 tells you that the brochure was published in January (the first month) of 1994. But the customer, not knowing your code, won't be able to figure out the publication date. And that's a good thing, since you don't want readers to think your brochure is dated.

If some of your brochures have similar titles, there may be confusion as to which brochure a prospect has requested. A coding system eliminates this confusion; when the customer requests "bulletin KS-9" you know precisely which piece of literature is wanted.

Some companies also like to add to the code number notation that indicates the number of copies printed and whether the brochure is from the original print run or a reprint. So the code SMB-1-5K could mean "static mixing brochure, first printing, 5,000 copies printed."

Under the code you should add a copyright notice, which should read "Copyright © 1994 by XYZ Corporation." If the brochure was printed in the United States, add in small type the text, "Printed in the U.S.A."

Is Promotional Literature Obsolete?

Computers, arcade games, and music video aside, print isn't dead yet, and won't be for some time. Book sales are up, magazine circulation increases every year, and more newspapers are published today than at any time since World War II. Microprocessors, optical disks, and micrographics haven't changed the fact that the printed page is still the most powerful medium for disseminating information about products, services, programs, causes, ideas, and organizations.

This is not to say that high-tech hasn't made its impact in the advertising world. Many new types of promotion are being tested every day. Among these you will find:

■ **Electronic catalogs**
Thanks to the combination of two-way interactive television and videotext, advertisers can now create electronic catalogs that are displayed on TV

screens. The electronic pages contain graphics and text and can blink, move, change color, and be combined with sound. The customer uses a control box or keypad to flip through the catalog; the keypad can also be used to order a product or request more information electronically.

■ Video brochures

Industrial manufacturers have been using films to supplement printed brochures for years. Now consumer companies are getting into the act. Many companies now put their sales pitches on videotape, and send these tapes to consumers as readily as they send printed brochures. Exercise equipment and other products that are easily demonstrated are ideal for this approach. And as VCR sales skyrocket, the use of the video brochure will increase.

■ Talking fliers

This technique has also been around for a while, but now is becoming more widespread. The advertiser puts the sales message on a small plastic record or a cassette tape, then mails it to the customer or binds the record into a magazine opposite a print ad for the product.

The more modern version of this is a piece of literature that contains a computer chip. When the brochure is opened, the chip produces sounds: music, spoken words, or both. This is a novel technique that gets attention and, although expensive, may be affordable for brochures used to sell big ticket items, if the production runs are modest (500 to 2,000 pieces).

■ Electronic mail

Reports, letters, and memos are now being sent over modems and telephone lines from one computer to another. Why not send price lists, product specifications, even computer-graphic drawings and promotional copy the same way? Advertisers may soon buy space on various electronic bulletin boards and database services to transmit promotional messages in electronic form. These same messages could also be contained in floppy diskettes mailed to customers or bound into the pages of a magazine.

■ Computer disks

Computer disks have been bound into ads, used as mailers, and incorporated into brochures. When inserted in your floppy disk drive, the promotional diskette takes you through a menu-driven, viewer-controlled sales presentation that combines text, computer graphics, and animation on screen.

■ Fax-on-demand

To fit in with today's fast-paced, in-a-rush society, more and more advertisers are designing sales literature intended to be transmitted by fax rather than mail. The designs avoid halftones and colors and are mostly line art and text, so that the literature, when faxed, is received in easy-to-read condition (halftones, shades of gray, and copy on colored backgrounds do not fax well). Some companies offer systems that automatically fax literature to prospects' fax machines without the need for human intervention.

New techniques and technologies should be tried, tested, and adopted if they work. But keep in mind that 99.9 percent of the promotional material in circulation today is made of ink and paper. The printed word still chronicles the history of the world, moves people to action, and sells billions of dollars worth of goods, services, and ideas. If you can master the skills required to produce great promotional literature, both you and your organization will prosper for years to come.

GLOSSARY

abscissa   The horizontal or *x*-axis of a graph.

airbrush   Artist's device for applying paint by means of a spray atomizer. Used for color illustration and photo retouching.

art   Illustrations and photographs used in promotional literature.

ASCII (American Standard Code for Information Interchange)   A standard code by which computers convert text into the numerical binary code that machines can understand. Pronounced "ask-key." Many desktop publishers, graphic designers, and typesetting bureaus require that your computer files be converted to ASCII so they can work with them on their equipment.

author's alterations   Changes made in the text of a sales piece after the type has been set.

backer card   Advertising poster designed to fit on a pole or product display rack.

back up   To print on the reverse side of a sheet of paper after printing on the front side.

balloon   White oval in a cartoon strip containing the character's dialogue and thoughts.

B&W   Black and white.

banner   Large advertising poster hung in store aisles and across the fronts of buildings.

bind   To mechanically join separate sheets of paper into a single piece of printed literature.

bleed   To print an illustration or photo to the edge of the page so that there is no margin.

blueline   Final proof of printing work. The blueline or "blue" is the advertiser's last chance to review the work before it is printed.

body copy   Main text of the brochure (as opposed to the headline, captions, or subheads).

boldface   Darker, thicker variation of a typeface.

broadside   Promotional flier that is folded for mailing.

brochure   Printed literature promoting a product, service, company, or idea.

budget   Amount of money the advertiser can afford to spend to produce the brochure.

bullet   Heavy dot used to draw attention to an item in the body copy or to separate items in a list.

bulletin   Printed literature providing news or information.

business reply mail   Envelope or card a prospect can mail back to the advertiser without affixing postage.

byline   Line below the title or at the end of a piece of writing giving the name of the author.

call-out   Words used to identify and explain elements shown in a picture. The words are connected by a line to the portion of the picture they describe.

campaign   Coordinated program of advertising, sales literature, direct mail, and other promotional activities.

caption   Text describing a photo or illustration.

catalog   Type of promotional literature containing descriptions of a number of different products.

circular   Printed advertising sheet featuring sale items and specials. Circulars are inserted in newspapers or packages or distributed by hand.

coated paper   Smoothly finished paper covered with a high-gloss coating. Used for an expensive look and for high-quality reproduction of color photography.

collateral   Brochures, booklets, and other printed promotional material.

color separations   Plates used for full-color printing. Usually, four plates are made: black, yellow, red, and blue.

color transparency   Color slide or overhead transparency.

comprehensive layout   Carefully drawn layout that shows what the finished page (e.g., of a brochure) will look like.

concept   General idea or theme of how to present a product or service to the consumer.

contact print   Small photographic print made by superimposing a negative on print paper. Contact prints are used to view a series of photographs and select the best ones for full-size reproduction and use in literature.

copyright   To register a piece of writing or art with the government so that it cannot be used by others without its author's permission.

corner card   Brief sentence or phrase printed on the outside of an envelope to entice the reader to open it and read the direct-mail piece inside.

cover stock   Stiff, heavy paper used for the covers of booklets ard brochures.

C print   Inexpensive print of a color photo. Used for review purposes rather than actual print production.

crop   To mark a photo so that undesired portions are deleted when the photo is reproduced in a brochure or booklet.

cut line   Photo caption.

depth of focus   Distance a photographer can move away from the subject while keeping it in focus.

design   To create the layout of an ad, brochure, or mailer.

desktop publishing   Electronic typesetting and page layout done using a desktop computer system.

desktop publishing software   Software programs that enable PC users to perform typesetting, page layout, illustration, design, and other graphic arts functions (traditionally done manually) at their desktop computers.

desktop publishing system   Hardware and software required to do desktop publishing. Usually consists of an IBM compatible or Macintosh personal computer with hard disk drive, page-layout software, and a laser printer.

die-cut   Special effect made by cutting out a portion of the cover (or any other page) of a brochure.

duotone   Process used to tint black-and-white photographs with a second color such as blue, red, or yellow.

electronic typesetting   Setting of camera-ready type using a desktop publishing system with a laser printer instead of a mechanical, photomechanical, or other traditional typesetting systems.

emboss   Special effect created by raising portions of a sheet of paper to form a design.

four-color   Material printed in full color using four different color inks (red, blue, yellow, black).

gatefold   Piece of paper folded twice vertically to form a six-page or six-panel brochure.

hard copy   Copy printed on paper using a computer printer, typewriter, or some other machine capable of producing type.

inquiry fulfillment literature   Brochures specifically designed to be sent to prospects who have asked for additional information on a particular product or service.

Mac   Short for Macintosh, a popular brand of personal computer used heavily for desktop publishing, especially in the graphics, advertising, and publishing industries.

MD (management discussion)   In an annual report, all the fine-print financial discussion and other details that appear in the back half of the report.

nixie   In direct mail, a mailing piece that is returned as undeliverable because the information on the mailing label is not current.

offset printing   Printing process in which the inked plate on the press does not come in contact with the printing paper but instead transfers, or offsets, its image to another cylinder, which then prints the image on the paper.

optical scanner   Device used to scan hard copy and convert the text to computer data so that it may be manipulated using desktop publishing or other computer systems used in the publishing process.

PageMaker   One of the most popular desktop publishing programs for page layout and design.

panel   In a booklet, pamphlet, or slim-jim brochure, one of the pages created when the sheet of paper is folded to form the brochure.

photostat   Reproduction of black-and-white line art on a glossy paper, suitable for direct reproduction by a printing press.

plus cover   In a brochure, a front and back cover of a heavier stock than is used for the inside pages. A "four-page plus cover" means four inside pages plus a four-page cover (outer front, inside front, inside back, outer back), which makes eight pages total.

prepress system   Refers to any system or operation, usually electronic, needed to convert text and layout into a format ready for printing on a printing press.

Quark   Another popular desktop publishing program that does page layouts and design.

rack-size brochure   Slim-jim brochure designed to be displayed on a literature rack (for example, travel and banking brochures).

sheetfed press or sheet press   Press into which the paper is fed in sheet format.

slim-jim   Brochure sized to fit folded into a number 10 business envelope.

specification sheet   Piece of sales literature that consists primarily of technical specifications and product features.

stock photo house   Company from which you can buy the right to reprint stock photos of various subjects in your sales literature.

tint   Light background of color on text or visuals. Used for emphasis and to highlight.

two color   Material printed in two colors, usually black and a second color such as red or blue.

varnish   Coating applied to color brochures to give photos, drawings, and other color material a shiny, sharper look. The varnish may be applied to the entire page or selectively to specific graphic elements on the page.

velox   Inexpensive black-and-white print of a photograph. Used primarily in layouts to show positioning of photos; not generally suited for direct reproduction on a printing press.

web press   Press that is fed paper in a continuous roll and in which the paper remains a continuous form until the printing process is complete and the paper is cut to produce individual brochures.

INDEX

ABOUT THE AUTHOR

Robert W. Bly is an independent copywriter and consultant specializing in industrial, high-tech, business-to-business, and direct response marketing.

He has written more than 500 brochures for numerous clients, including Brooklyn Union Gas, Chemical Bank, Associated Air Freight, AlliedSignal, CoreStates Financial Corporation, On-Line Software, and ITT Fluid Technology.

Mr. Bly is the author of 25 books including *The Copywriter's Handbook* (Henry Holt & Co.) and *Business-to-Business Direct Marketing* (NTC Business Books), and has been published in such magazines as *Amtrak Express*, *Cosmopolitan*, *New Jersey Monthly*, *Writer's Digest*, *Computer Decisions*, *Direct Marketing*, and *Business Marketing*. He is a member of the Business Marketing Association and the American Institute of Chemical Engineers.

Questions and comments on *The Perfect Sales Piece* may be sent to:

Bob Bly
Copywriter/Consultant
22 E. Quackenbush Avenue, 3rd Floor
Dumont, NJ 07628
(201) 385-1220